Bryan Scant is a Partner and Resolution-accredited specialist in financial remedies, based on the South Coast. He has particular expertise in cases involving public sector pensions, with a strong focus on the armed forces. Bryan regularly advises both service members and their families, navigating the unique complexities of these pension schemes.

A collaboratively trained practitioner, Bryan is committed to resolving disputes outside of court wherever possible, using non-court dispute resolution (NCDR) methods. He has a particular interest in hybrid mediation, assisting clients seeking constructive and efficient outcomes in a non-confrontational manner.

Bryan also contributed to the second edition of the Pension Advisory Group (PAG) report and the Advicenow guide to pensions on divorce, reflecting his commitment to improving understanding and practice in this evolving area of law.

A Practical Guide to Pensions on Divorce for Lawyers

Second Edition

A Practical Guide to Pensions on Divorce for Lawyers

Second Edition

Bryan Scant LLB (Hons)

Law Brief Publishing

Published 2025 by Law Brief Publishing, an imprint of Law Brief Publishing Ltd
30 The Parks
Minehead
Somerset
TA24 8BT

www.lawbriefpublishing.com

Paperback: 978-1-918241-09-9

PREFACE

This book is correct as of 30th September 2025. This is an ever-evolving area of law, and specialist advice should always be obtained where pensions are a feature of a case as the legal approach can, and does, change over time.

Bryan Scant
October 2025

CONTENTS

Chapter One	Introduction	1
Chapter Two	Different Types of Orders	9
Chapter Three	Completing Financial Disclosure	15
Chapter Four	Instructing a PODE	25
Chapter Five	Offsetting and Ringfencing Pre/Post-Marital Pensions	41
Chapter Six	Uniformed Services and Public Sector Pensions	61
Chapter Seven	McCloud	71
Chapter Eight	Conclusion	77

CHAPTER ONE

INTRODUCTION

Pensions are a daunting asset for many financial remedy practitioners. They are complex, often unknown and often create a feeling of anxiety that advising on them could cross that line between legal advice and financial advice. It is also an area that is not well understood by many, and not an area that those at the early stages of their career are often taught on their journey to qualification. Even those with many years' experience and their own pension provision find the asset a confusing one to deal with.

Historically, many pensions were linked to a pension member's salary (final salary/defined benefit schemes). These schemes for those in the private sector are few and far between now, largely owing to the cost of maintaining such an expensive pension scheme. The result is that fewer of us are involved in those schemes, or understand their rules, calculations or the benefits that they provide.

For many, their pensions are in defined contribution/money purchase schemes. That is what most people are familiar with; they have a pot of money invested on their behalf, waiting patiently for retirement. With those pensions, what you see is what you get in many respects when it comes to their value.

When it came to divorce, until 1995, with the introduction of pension attachment order (also known as "earmarking orders"), your pension truly was your own on divorce. A pension-member spouse may have had a maintenance obligation, indirectly reducing their available pension income, or an order obligating the pension trustees to pay a percentage of the pension to the non-member spouse. A pension was secure, untouchable, and always in the name of the member-spouse until their death. However as with many aspects of family law, times have changed, and the law has evolved to cater for changing attitudes. The law was not fit for purpose and reform was required to avoid the non-member spouse losing out on pension benefits and an income on divorce, or in the case of attachment order, on the death of the member-spouse. After all, after a 30-year marriage, why should the recipient lose their retirement income because of the member-spouse's death post-divorce? That was the risk and reality for many prior to the introduction of Pension Sharing Orders.

The Welfare Reforms and Pensions Act 1999 introduced Pension Sharing Orders for proceedings issued after 1 December 2000. For the first time, this enabled the court to take a percentage of a spouse's pension (the member spouse) and transfer it out of their name and into the name of the other spouse (the non-member spouse). This facilitated a pension asset to be shared on divorce in a way that had not been possible previously, reducing the pension pot of the member spouse and giving the non-member spouse a pension credit in their own name independent of the member spouse's. In certain circumstances this can be invested in an entirely independent pension product, or in the case of some defined benefit pension schemes, such as the armed forces, a new pension pot in the non-member's spouse's name within the same scheme.

It is not uncommon for a client to make contact and enquire about splitting a pension on separation, without divorcing. This is more common in those cases that are amicable or where they are in less of a rush to formally divorce and are instead looking at a separation agreement. It is also a feature of religious separations where the parties do not wish to formally divorce and instead opt for a judicial separation. Many unmarried couples will also experience an initial level of anxiety at the prospect of losing their pension, a common misconception that ties into the myth of "common law spouse". It is only on divorce that the court can make a pension sharing order, and not on the back of a separation agreement, as is often misunderstood by clients.

It is also important to note that on a judicial separation application, the court cannot make a pension sharing order. in those instances, an ongoing periodical payments order may be necessary.

The issue that has since arisen is, how do we as practitioners treat pensions in a financial remedy cases? For many practitioners, it was drummed into us at university and beyond that we have to be exceptionally careful that we are not giving regulated financial advice. The consequence for doing so is not only negligent, but potentially criminal as providing regulated financial advice and not being regulated by the FCA is a criminal offence. This leave practitioners dancing a fine line between advising a client on their pensions in the context of a divorce, without going over that line and into the remit of giving advice that only a regulated financial advisor should be providing. Practitioners should always have this at the forefront of their mind when advising on pension on divorce, as clients often find information online that we know to be incorrect but are not permitted to tell them for fear of giving financial advice.

The first point that must be made is this: always signpost you client to a financial advisor. As practitioners in an increasingly litigious world, we should ensure that our clients have been given that recommendation, especially when it comes to what do with a pension credit. Ideally, the involvement of a financial advisor in the matter at an early stage is sensible way ahead, especially those with larger pensions where the income exceeds their needs, or their pension income pushed them into a higher tax bracket and sharing of a pension can be a tax efficient way of managing their assets. Knowing when to work with other professionals is commonplace, and the need for the input of a Pension on Divorce Expert (PODE) is now readily understood, the same should be said for financial advisors.

Pensions are not an easy topic to understand. The terminology is sometimes alien and complex, what it means in practice even more so. The pension freedoms brought in by the Pension Schemes Act 2015 do not help make this area easier, as people now have the ability to take a significant portion of their pension as a cash lump sum from age 55 (increasing to 57 in April 2028), removing it completely from the pension pot and available to spend as they please, or in the worse cases, dissipate to try and frustrate a spouse's claim. This of course has its consequences; the tax liability can be steep for those who takes more than 25% of their pension. Beware of this, some client's may think that removing money from their pension to pay their former spouse a lump sum by way of offsetting is a potential solution, however it could have significant tax consequences that the client has not foreseen. Ensure that a financial advisor provides the correct advice on this before committing any proposals like this to paper.

Of course, it would be impossible to write about pensions on divorce without referencing the Pension Advisory Group's second report on the treatment of Pensions on divorce[1] (PAG 2). All practitioners who are involved in the financial remedy proceedings should read this report and look on it as an essential guide for family

1 Pension Advisory Group, (2024) A Guide to the Treatment of Pensions on Divorce, Nuffield Foundation

practitioners when it comes to pensions, especially in light of the case law which reaffirms the significance of the report as a tool for practitioners. The first iteration of the PAG report was published in 2019 and was a ground-breaking cross-profession report which reviewed the vast area of pensions on divorce and produced for the first time a comprehensive guide on how pensions should be treated. Contributors to the report included some of the most pre-eminent names in family law from solicitor and barristers to members of the judiciary; alongside pension actuaries and financial advisors. HHJ Hess stated in W v H [2020][2] that the report was "prima facie persuasive", giving the report judicial approval as a resource on the subject. He later re-affirmed this in SP v AL [2024].

That cross-profession publication contains a wealth of information and guidance for practitioners. The report was subsequently updated in 2024 with the publication of a second edition. In the interests of full transparency, the author was a member of the second pension advisory group and was a contributor to the second report.

When it comes to the types of pensions. they are generally separated into 2 types – defined benefit and defined contribution pensions.

Defined contribution pensions have a variety of names, including money purchase pensions, stakeholder pensions or personal pensions. These types of pensions are valued based on the money that has been paid into the pot, and the fund value is often sufficient to provide the necessary information for a Form E and thereafter a PODE instruction, if required. The money in the pension is

2 Hess HJ, W v H (divorce : financial remedies) [2020] EWFC B1 para 59

invested by the pension provider until retirement or the exercise of the party's pension freedoms under the 2015 legislation.

Defined benefit pensions are usually pensions from an employer and based on a pension members' salary. These also go by the name of final salary pensions or career average earnings (CARE), depending on the type. These pensions are less common in the private sector now than they once were, but nevertheless they are still out there and do present themselves in divorce cases, especially parties with older pensions. The most common scenarios where these pensions still feature are cases involving employment within the NHS and uniformed services such as the armed forces, Police and Fire Service. In the circumstances where a party is employed by the public sector, this should immediately alert a practitioner to the likely issue of pensions, and the need for expert input.

Pensions are often an asset that is ignored by parties. It is extremely common for a party to instruct a solicitor and say that they "aren't interested in pensions, we keep our own", or "we've agreed not to touch each other's pensions". This could be a mistake and one that should be corrected at an early opportunity. Pensions are a valuable asset, and it is imperative that they are properly considered. Many clients will choose to focus on the immediate cash assets without appreciating the importance of also looking at future pension income. In an age of "silver separators" it is especially important to ensure that the financially weaker party is protected in their later years as those cases often feature scenarios whereby a career, and in turn pension accrual, has been sacrificed in favour of the other party's, be that to maintain the home or to bring up the children. That loss of pension contribution is a factor that should be considered on divorce. The court made clear some years ago that a homemaker's contribution was just as equal as any bread winner's contribution, but that will extend to pensions also.

A further common scenario that we are all likely to have heard is the focus on the house, with one party wanting to keep the house in lieu of a claim against the other's pension. In financial remedy cases, this is known as offsetting where a party keeps cash assets instead of sharing pension assets. This can be a false economy and not something that should be considered without proper advice and guidance from both a PODE for the offsetting calculation and a financial advisor to consider future income and expenditure needs. This is the old adage of comparing apples and pears, 2 different types of asset that are being spoken of as if they are equals. Remember, a pound in a pension is not the same as a pound in your pocket or in property. Further, the party retaining the house has to maintain and run it in the future. If they experience a sudden drop in their income when they retire, that may not be possible. A pension sharing order may help remedy this.

It would be wrong to assume that only high value cases will involve complicated pension assets. On the contrary, it is often the low to mid-value cases that require complex analysis of these difficult assets. Take a nurse, for example, who has worked 20 years for the NHS. There may be a house with a reasonable sum of equity, limited savings, but a significant defined benefit pension scheme in the NHS which will provide a cash lump sum on retirement, and an index linked guaranteed pension income for life. That pension scheme is going to feature as an important factor in a case and will add to the time and cost to the client of resolving the financial aspects of the divorce. There is a much greater awareness of this than there once was, but many people find the issue of pensions particularly difficult to comprehend as they very much see it as their own asset that should not be shared.

A further issue is the perception that a pension is their own individual asset as it resulted from one party's employment. Other, more realisable assets generated during the marriage appear not to (usually) have the same attitude attributed to them, but one of the first points to make to a party on divorce is that a pension, irrespective of when it was accrued, is an asset that must be considered on divorce. The law dictates that all assets are considered on divorce, albeit the extent of that treatment will of course turn on the facts of the case, but nevertheless a party has a obligation to comply with their duty of full and frank financial disclosure and that extends to providing a CETV (cash equivalent transfer value) of their pension. This is still applicable in those cases where pensions are not being shared, for example in instances where parties have mediated and agreed that due to their age or significant and unmatched pre-marital contributions their pensions are not being shared, they still must provide a valuation on their D81. A CETV should therefore be requested at the earliest opportunity.

Advicenow have produced a free online guide to the treatment of pensions on divorce which practitioners may wish to consider signposting their clients to for easy-to-read guidance on the process from an independent source. The guide goes through the divorce process and is written for those without legal knowledge, which can be a helpful resource especially for those where they do not have means to instruct solicitors to provide comprehensive advice, or for mediators who are not able to provide advice to the parties.

It is intended that this book will serve as a practical guide to family practitioners who are finding themselves dealing with the evolving world of pensions on divorce. It will give you a steer as to what information to obtain from your client, how to complete the Form E, and how the court will subsequently deal with that pension asset, which in itself is a continuously evolving field of law, as will become apparent.

CHAPTER TWO

DIFFERENT TYPES OF ORDERS

There are a number of different orders available to parties who are divorcing. These are:

- Pension sharing orders

- Pension attachments orders (previously known as "earmarking")

A pension sharing order is now the most common form of pension order made on divorce. Where a pension sharing order is made, a percentage of the member spouse's pension is removed from the pot in their name and transferred into a pension pot in the other party's name. Using the wording of the precedent consent orders, the pension debit member is the spouse who has the pension asset, and the pension credit member is the spouse receiving the pension credit.

What happens with that pension credit is very dependent on the type of scheme and the financial advice given to the pension credit member. Some schemes, such as the armed forces schemes, will not allow a pension credit to be transferred out of an armed forces scheme. In those cases, the pension credit member will have their own standalone pension pot within the Armed Forces Pension Scheme, entirely separate to the member spouses. With certain schemes, it is not possible to transfer out from that scheme and the pension credit member must have their own pot within that scheme. This is known as an internal transfer. Future pension accrual for the member spouse will accrue in their sole name and will not have an impact on the pension credit member's pot.

In contrast, some schemes will not permit an internal transfer and will insist that the pension credit is transferred out of their scheme and into an entirely new scheme in the pension credit member's name. In those cases, it is important that the pension credit member receives financial advice so that they can make an informed decision on where to invest their pension credit. Practitioners cannot and must not advise on what to do with a pension credit, financial advice should instead be sought. The pension credit member will need to inform the pension provider of where the pension credit will be transferred so that the pension sharing order can be properly implemented.

The pension sharing annex at section F provides the option to elect for an internal or external transfer, but this is optional and should not be completed without financial advice, even if the scheme only allows one type of transfer. This was a central issue to the case of *T v T (Variation of a Pension Sharing Order and underfunded schemes) [2021] EWFC B67* and HHJ Hess made it clear in his judgement that he endorsed the wording in the initial PAG report, reaffirmed in paragraph V.43 of PAG 2, that practitioners should not tick either box on the pension sharing annex for this could be considered providing regulated financial advice.

Pension sharing orders are dealt with using percentages, to 2 decimal places. This does make matters slightly more complex as you begin by asking the client to obtain a valuation of the pension, you look at the capital value and/or income it generates, but the pension sharing order itself is dealt with as a percentage. Whilst practitioners are familiar with this, for many clients they find this an unusual complexity and will frequently refer to the pension and any sharing order in monetary values. It is important to remember that because a pension sharing order is dealt with as a percentage, the actual monetary value of a pension sharing order may change between the date that a CETV is provided or a PODE report is prepared, and the date that it is implemented. There could even be a change between the date an order is received from the court and the date that the order is implemented. The reason for this is that a pension can change in value due to fluctuations in the value of investments or changes in the pension members' pensionable service, and clients should be aware of this. The pension sharing order will take effect on the transfer day, which is determined by the pension scheme administrator. The calculation of the pension share is based on the value of the pension on the valuation day, as specified in the pension sharing annex. Once the pension provider receives all required documentation—including the sealed court order, annex, and any applicable fees—they have up to four months to implement the order. The pension share is calculated as of the valuation day, but the actual value may fluctuate during the four-month implementation period.

Pension attachment orders are a different, and rarer, pension order that can be made by the courts. These pre-date pension sharing orders and were implemented by the Pensions Act 1995. The difference between a pension sharing order and a pension attachment order is that a pension attachment order does not remove a pension credit from the member spouse's pension, instead the order "attaches" to the member's pension. The pension company pay an amount of the member spouse's pension to the non-member spouse directly, without needing to be paid by the pension member themselves as if it were a maintenance order. These orders are again expressed as a percentage, and that percentage of the members pension is paid. These payments only come into payment when the member spouse retires and receives their pension income.

The downside of a pension attachment order is that the pension remains entirely in the name of the member spouse. They can elect when to retire and receive that income, which means they could defer retirement and receipt of the pension income to try and frustrate the non-member's claims. The order also dies with the member spouse, so on their death the pension stops being paid to the non-member spouse. In cases where there is a significant age gap or where the member spouse may have health issues the limit life expectancy, there is a risk that the non-member spouse may only receive the income for a limited period of time, if at all.

A further issue to be aware of is the tax consequences of an attachment order. As the pension remains the pension of the member spouse in its entirety, the income that is generated by it is taxed at the rate that the member spouse pays. If the member spouse pays higher rate tax, the pension income is taxed accordingly and the non-member spouse, assuming they are a lower rate taxpayer, loses out. Before considering a pension attachment order, financial advice should be sought to ensure then non-member spouse fully understands the consequences of these types of order.

A pension attachment order will also end on the non-member spouse's re-marriage, whereas a pension sharing order will create an entirely independent pension pot that is not affected by death of the member spouse or re-marriage.

Finally, the Matrimonial Causes Act provides for the court to look to achieve a clean break where possible. A pension attachment order runs contrary to that principle as there is still a financial connection between the parties. A pension attachment order is capable of variation as well, so it could result in further litigation and potentially a change in the non-member spouse's income later in life. Pension attachment orders should be used with caution, in light of the ability for a pension to be shared by way of a pension sharing order, that may be the more appropriate means of guaranteeing a future income for your client. In practice, pension attachment orders are now rare and pension sharing orders have become the preferred means of sharing a pension on divorce.

It is possible to vary a pension attachment order and "replace" it with a pension sharing order to achieve a clean break and avoid the pitfalls above of pension attachment orders. the process for varying a pension attachment order is dealt with using the fast-track procedure and will likely require the input of a PODE to properly calculate the percentage of the pension required to achieve the same level of income envisaged by the pension attachment order. Do not overlook the tax consequences here, if the pension is now being paid to the non-member spouse as a member of the pension scheme, they may pay a different level of tax that could result in a different net monthly amount being received by the recipient than was intended. If a PODE is instructed, check the report to see whether the report is based on gross figures or whether any assumptions have been made for income tax. Consider again the involvement of a financial advisor to advise on the potential tax consequences and whether that may have an impact on the recipient.

CHAPTER THREE

COMPLETING FINANCIAL DISCLOSURE

It would appear logical that we start at the beginning of a client's legal journey and consider what we should do first, before we even begin considering what to do with the information that we obtain.

The first step when taking instructions is to identify whether there are pensions involved in a case. As set out above, some professions will automatically alert a practitioner to the existence of a pension by their very nature. For example, a client employed by the NHS will automatically raise the question of whether there is an NHS pension to consider, as will be the case with any serving or former member of the armed forces.

You are going to require a formal valuation from the pension company for each pension. This is the Cash Equivalent Transfer Value (CETV), which can either be requested by the client directly or by the solicitor through sending the provider form P duly completed and signed. Providing a signed Form P to the pension provider will ensure that the correct pension information is provided early on. The information can then be used to populate the Form E and later provided to the PODE for them to prepare the report.

Most pension providers will provide a free CETV once in a 12-month period though If your client is currently in receipt of their pension then they may have to pay a fee for this information. It is not uncommon for this fee to be quite sizeable depending on the pension and the pension provider. Some pension providers, Veterans UK on behalf of the MOD for example, will provide a basic CETV of a member's pension for free. However, to obtain further information for the purpose of a divorce will require the member to pay a fee. This more detailed CETV will include dates of service/contribution to the pension scheme and the information required to complete a Form E. Whilst more cost sensitive clients may be concerned about having to pay this fee, it may work out more cost effective to apply for it at the outset than have to go back and obtain it later if the correct information is not obtained.

It is good practice to advise a client to obtain a CETV at the outset. If you are being instructed on the finances then you will need this information at some point in the future, either to submit a consent order and D81 to the court or for formal proceedings. Some pension providers can take a long time to provide a CETV, another reason to make the request sooner rather than later. The NHS for example has previously had a reputation for taking a long time to provide the necessary information for a Form E, so if you are acting in a matter with an NHS pension it is important to request this information as soon as possible so that there is no unnecessary delay.

It is not unheard of for a party to refuse to provide pension information, especially those who know they have a healthy pension pot that they are reluctant to share. In those rare instances, judicial involvement may be necessary to make an order permitting the non-member spouse (or their representative) to submit Form P on the member's behalf. If this is required, ensure that there is permission in the order to disclose a copy of the order to the pension provider so that they are aware of why this request is coming from the non-member, and why the member has not signed the Form P themselves. An application for this should be made in form D11 with a draft order and an explanation of why this is required.

When it comes to completing the Form E, it is important that the relevant section of the Form E is completed properly. It is also important that when you receive a Form E from the other party or their solicitor, it is properly compared and contrasted with the CETV documents provided in support. If CETVs are not provided with a Form E, it is essential that they are requested as soon as possible and ideally prior to an FDA so that due consideration can be given to whether an expert instruction is necessary. Not only is this necessary for the proper compliance with a party's ongoing duty of financial disclosure, but the relevant section of the Form E is also the information that the court will have before it when being asked to consider whether the instruction of an PODE is necessary. Further, a PODE will require a formal CETV before they can began preparing their report.

After exchange of disclosure, factors to look out for when reviewing a Form E include:

1. What type of pension is it? Defined benefit/money purchase?

2. The value

3. Whether the pension is in payment

4. When was the CETV calculated?

Addressing each point in turn:

1. The type of pension is important. Ensure that the type of pension listed on the Form E correlates with the type of

pension disclosed on the CETV documentation from the pension provider. It is not uncommon for mistakes to be made in drafting Forms E, either using software that auto populates the fields on a Form E, or where parties have drafted the Form E themselves. Do not rely solely on what is in the Form E, check what the pension provider says the type of pension is, for example a Form E could say "occupational pension", implying it could be a defined contribution scheme, but the CETV from the pension provider instead identifies the pension as being a defined benefit pension. Identifying a pension early will flag up whether the input of a PODE is necessary.

2. The value of the pension is, obviously, important. The Cash Equivalent Transfer Value is defined by The Pensions Regulator as *"the expected cost of providing the member's benefits within the scheme."*. When considering a defined contribution pension, this is usually the total of the contributions and the growth of the invested capital. With a defined benefit CETV, The Pensions Regulator describes this as "*a value determined on actuarial principles, which requires assumptions to be made about the future course of events affecting the scheme and the member's benefits*". This should be seen as a strong indication that the input of a PODE is necessary. This is also a good indication of a valuable asset that you should not overlook when dividing the assets.

3. Is the pension in payment? If so, consideration should be given to what level of income it produces, what impact a pension sharing order would have as well as it then formulating what position you should or could advance when trying to pursue or rebut a claim for a pension sharing

order. A pension in payment also often triggers the provider charging for a CETV, which can be a significant fee. There is also the consideration of what impact a pension sharing order may have on a party's ability to meet their needs. If they are retired and their pension is the only source of income, consideration must be given to how both parties will meet needs in retirement. It may also be the case that notwithstanding the pension, there are other available assets with which to meet needs.

4. As previously mentioned, the date that the CETV is calculated is important. Generally, a CETV is valid for 12 months, however there may be circumstances where it is either necessary or advantageous to request a further CETV. The first check is that the CETV is dated within the previous 12 months. If it is not, then it may be sensible to request a further CETV. If you are approaching an FDA and the CETV is shortly going to be 12 months old, then it may be necessary to include as a direction at the FDA provision for a revised CETV. If a PODE is being instructed and the CETV has expired by the time the letter of instruction has been sent, then the PODE is likely to request one to complete the report. It is sensible to diarise the expiration of a CETV. Some matters face delays due to failed negotiations, court delays or the time spent drafting and finessing a letter of instruction, which means that time will rapidly disappear. If you realise too late that a new CETV will be required, then you may find the FDR needing to be re-listed due the PODE being unable to finalise their report. PODEs will insist on an in-date CETV being provided with the LOI.

It may be necessary to consider raising questions on pension disclosure once Forms E are exchanged. If you are considering disclosure from a party who has had a varied career with multiple employments, for example, but has only disclosed one pension, it may require further examination. Discuss with your client what conversations the parties had about it during the marriage. Were conversations had about that brief spell working for the NHS prior to marriage? Or that "forgotten" pension from a period of employment prior to the marriage? Consider whether the disclosed pensions are what you might expect from the party given their age, level of seniority in their career and their general approach to finances. For example, does the financially prudent husband with various investments, bank account and organised finances not also save into a pension? It is also prudent to consider payslips and examine whether pension deductions are taken from the party's salary. Some payslips will state the pension provider, e.g. Standard Life, whereas others may be more vague. Cross reference the CETV provided with the narrative on the payslip and check they match. Look also at the CETV, do not assume that the CETV provided is for the current employment. Some CETVs will include dates that the party contributed to the pension, giving a clear indication of whether it is the current pension. Some also include a breakdown of all payments made into the pension, a further way of checking any gaps. If you continue to be unsure as to whether all pensions have been disclosed, consider an online search for the party. Their LinkedIn profile may disclose employment that would prompt a query on whether a pension was provided by a previous employer. That is a very cautious and detailed approached, but in cases where lack of trust is an issue it may be a sensible exercise. Many also "forget" that they had other pensions, so raising a question about it in their questionnaire may serve to jog their memory. There are also many instances where a pension was non-contributory, resulting in a party genuinely not being aware of the existence of the pension. It is not an unreasonable request to ask a party to make enquiries of and provide evidence that they have properly looked into whether a pension is in existence.

In future, the creation of the Pensions Dashboard Programme will help alleviate this issue with the advent of a single online platform where anyone can access their pension information from all providers in a single place, removing the uncertainty over pension disclosure. This programme will also enable a party to identify any missing pensions that may have been lost over time and ensure greater transparency and, it is hoped, less issue of one party questioning the other's disclosure when it comes to pension assets.

In low-income cases it would not necessarily be unusual for a party to have opted out of paying into a pension in order to have more take home cash each month. Auto enrolment into workplace pensions was brought in by the Pensions Act 2008. This has required all employers to provide employees with a pension, gradually extending from larger employers initially, to all employers now. An employee can opt-out, just because their employer provides the pension does not mean that they were part of it. If a party has opted out, ask for evidence of this from them. An employer has to provide an employee who asks to opt-out of their pension with an "opt-out notice", which should be requested in a questionnaire if that position is being advanced by a party. A party's employer ought to be able to provide this if requested.

Proportionality is important to bear in mind. As lawyers it could be said that we are not acting in a client's best interests if we pursue an unreasonable case, or expend significant sums on a disproportionate asset base. We have all reads the Judgements where costs are criticised and have all likely heard the warnings from a District Judge when looking at the figures on a Form H at a hearing.

There are other factors to consider when looking at a defined benefit scheme, such as a uniformed service pension or NHS. As a defined benefit pension can be based on final salary or average earnings a promotion could result in an increase in the value of the pension as income has increased. If you know that the pension member has recently been promoted, then it may be prudent to request a revised CETV. Similarly, if a uniformed services pension member has passed the point at which their pension could be paid immediately upon retirement, then that could also prompt an increase in the value of the CETV. Remember that retirement in the context of a public sector pension is not always the same as state retirement age and the individual scheme rules should be checked. The CETV should be checked against the dates of service in those circumstances, and the relevant rules of the pension scheme. It could be the case that a pension member will receive their pension earlier than the non-member spouse will under the rules of the pension scheme, which results in an income gap where one party is in receipt of their pension, but the other has many years to wait.

Once you have exchanged disclosure, consider whether the instruction of a PODE is necessary. A PODE report is a worthwhile investment and are important in order to consider the proper division of pensions in certain cases. Many couples make decisions not to invest in pensions, choosing instead to invest their money in buy to let properties for example, and in those cases where the pension assets are relatively small defined contribution schemes, a Judge may not agree with a request to instruct a PODE. However, if the pensions involve a defined benefit scheme, either public or private sector, then serious consideration should be given to the instruction of a PODE. In cases with a uniformed service pension it also always necessary to instruct a PODE to properly advise.

PAG 2 sets out examples of cases where it would be necessary to instruct a PODE in part 6 (para 6.10 and 6.11) and practitioners should ensure that they have read and are familiar with these recommendations.

Further, firms may have obligations under their professional indemnity insurance to instruct a PODE where pensions are valued over a certain amount.

If a client refuses to agree to the instruction of a PODE, contrary to clear advice, it is good practice to ask them to sign a disclaimer confirming that they have been advised to instruct a PODE and have chosen to proceed without. Remember, without that expert input it not possible to properly advise a client on the correct treatment of the pension assets.

On receipt of the non-member spouse's Form E, look at their income needs and compare that to the member spouse's Form E. Are their income needs less than 50% of the pension income as projected in the Form E or as it in payment? If so, this may assist discussions about ring-fencing pre-marital pensions where you can submit that there is enough pension income to meet needs and therefore consider the sharing principal and the question of non-matrimonial property, which will be further addressed below in the context of SP v Al and Standish. When preparing your client's Form E, consider the outgoings schedule and whether there is sufficient income to meet needs based on a future reduction in pension income post-pension sharing. Do not overlook at that an outgoings schedule is a party's income need **net**, whereas the income figures in a CETV or in a PODE report are usually **gross.**

It may be the case that a pension sharing order could reduce the income tax payable and result in less of a reduction in net income than would appear to be the case on paper, though appropriate advice from a financial advisor and/or tax specialist should be obtained to confirm this.

CHAPTER FOUR

INSTRUCTING A PODE

Consider the instruction of a PODE at an early stage in a case. Not only from a practical point of view in terms of when you need to instruct, but also from the perspective of advising your client.

When first instructed on a financial matter and you make enquiries of your client as to what pension assets there may be, it would be prudent to warn them that a PODE may be required. A PODE report can cost thousands, and it is a disbursement that a client should be advised on at the earliest opportunity to manage their expectations and ensure that they are able to budget accordingly. For many clients with pensions that require a PODE input, such as uniformed services personnel, the pension could be one of it not the biggest asset in the case. A public sector pension will be steadfastly held on to by a member, often unwilling to comprehend sharing it, let alone instructing a PODE at significant expense. In those instances, an explanation that a pension sharing order is likely to be ordered by the court and the instruction of a PODE is necessary to ensure that the correct amount of pension is shared. If pension sharing is inevitable, it is important that the correct amount is shared. Calculations done on the back of an envelope are wholly inappropriate and could cost the pension member significantly more than it should. PAG 2 notes at para 6.11 that *"Whatever their ages, where one of the parties has a significant public or private sector Defined Benefit scheme CE, equal division of CE can lead to very unexpected outcomes and such cases will require PODE input. When considering Defined Benefit pensions in a needs case, above £200,000 (measured by CE), it would usually be the case that a PODE report will be necessary."* Other examples of when a PODE is requires are detailed in this section of the guide.

Many clients want their divorce concluded yesterday and instructing a PODE is not going to enable matters to move swiftly, but it is important to have correct professional input when required. A PODE report is a complex matter that requires time and specialist input. PODEs are highly qualified for a reason - their task is not straightforward. Often, depending on the pension scheme, it is not just the time that it takes for the PODE to undertake their task, but you are reliant on pension providers complying with requests for information to enable the actuary to complete their report. The data gathering stage can be as lengthy as the report writing and should be factored in. Some providers are better than others and provide information swiftly, others can take a significant period to provide information to the PODE to enable them to even start their report. Bear this in mind when providing timescales to a client or drafting your FDA Order and timetabling the next stages in proceedings. It is easy to assume that a PODE only needs a few weeks from receipt of the order to producing their report, however it would be sensible to include additional time into the court timetable to cater for unexpected delays.

In voluntary proceedings, contact the other party's solicitor and explain that you consider it a necessary step in the process. Not only are you protecting your client and ensuring that the division of the pension is fair, but you are also protecting yourself as a practitioner.

Obtain quotes from PODEs as if you were preparing a Part 25 application together with CVs and timescales. Different PODEs will work to different timescales, and some require more input from clients than others. Many experienced practitioners will have a

PODE of choice that they often instruct. As a general rule, it is good practice to ensure that the PODE is suitably qualified and subscribes to the PAG report's views as that has been accepted as good practice, especially since the endorsement in *W v H (divorce: financial remedies)* and subsequent case law. Appendix D of PAG 2 contains a recommendation that a PODE self certifies, with a number of points listed therein.

A further consideration is how much work will be required by the client vs how much will the PODE be able to undertake. Some PODEs make it a term of their instruction that the parties obtain information from pension providers themselves, which is suitable for those who are organised and comfortable with contacting pension providers themselves. Not all are, and in those cases, it may be more appropriate to instruct a PODE who will ask for a signed form of authority and obtain the necessary data themselves. That is often reflected in their fee understandably, so be aware of that.

Consider also the costs of the solicitor acting as the conduit between the PODE and the client. Whilst the actuary may be more expensive if they data gather themselves; costs could easily increase through receiving a request from the PODE, forwarding that to your client, obtaining the information, checking it is what was asked for and then sending to the PODE. When it comes to some public sector pensions the information is publicly available online for the PODE to obtain, which means that this may not be as great a concern in those cases.

When it comes to considering the timescale, look at the wording of the estimate and terms. Is it 8 weeks from receipt of all the information? Or is it 8 weeks from receipt of the letter of instruction? The 2 can be vastly different, depending on how long the data gathering takes. When you are involving third party pension providers you become dependent on their timescales in addition to those of the actuary. Whilst not as important in voluntary negotiations, it is still an important consideration especially if the client is keen that matters progress swiftly.

In court proceedings, the usual practice is to request permission to instruct an actuary at the First Appointment. Obtain the relevant information from the potential PODE first, costs, timescale etc, in advance. Not only is this needed to comply with your Part 25 obligations when requesting the instruction of an expert, but it also saves time and makes the FDA more efficient. It would also be sensible, and again in compliance with Part 25 obligations, to have prepared a draft LOI or at the very least be prepared with the proposed questions of the PODE. The more detail the better so that the FDA order can be drafted as succinctly as possible, and the court provided with the necessary information.

Whilst it would still be a positive step to have agreed the identity of the expert at the FDA and included their details in the order, the order should also set out what you are asking the expert to do and if possible, the calculations that will be required. Should some aspects be left to be determined after, for example if it is agreed to instruct an expert to calculate income in retirement, it would be useful to also set out on which party's retirement, with a proposed date, to avoid later correspondence trying to determine that. If an agreement cannot be reached then the court can be asked to decide on that point there and then, without needing to seek judicial guidance later, potentially wasting several weeks going back and forth in correspondence, as well as incurring further costs. It would be useful to determine the following at the FDA:

- Identity of the PODE

- Timescales
- Calculation date
- Scope of instruction, including whether offsetting is included
- Date range for pension accrual – all pension accrual or relationship accrual, for example
- The equalisation date for the calculations. The fewer the dates, the better

Generally, the FDA order will provide for the letter of instruction to be agreed within a set time frame after the FDA, often 7 days. The more details agreed or ordered by the court at he FDA, the less problematic this aspect of the process. The vaguer the court order the more there is to dispute after the hearing. 7 days is not a long time when you consider that there are likely other directions to be complied with in that time scale. This is a further reason why a draft letter of instruction is a sensible step in first appointment preparation.

The PAG report provides very useful guidance on the instruction of a PODE, including a template letter of instruction that can be adapted to the parties' needs. The letter of instruction should set out the background to the matter, such as dates of birth, dates of marriage etc. If there are various date ranges being reported on, such as dates of cohabitation or dates or marriage, to decree absolute/final divorce order or separation, then this should clearly be set out in the letter. It should also set out the respective parties' pensions. The key element of the letter of instruction is the nature of the PODE's instruction. What is it that you are asking the actuary to do? It is not as simple as sending them the pension information and asking the PODE to tell lawyers or the court what to do, the PODE is only going to answer questions put to them with any decision about how pensions are divided being a matter for the parties in discussions or the court.

In cases involving uniformed service schemes it is essential to also include that party's anticipated date for leaving the service. This has an important impact on their pension and leaving this information out could lead to an incorrect assumption being made about that party's income in retirement, resulting in an incorrect amount of the pension being shared.

Health information, if relevant, should also be included. Most PODEs will ask for a health questionnaire to be completed if that is a potential factor in their report as it may impact life expectancy and in turn alter the annuity rates for parties with defined contribution pensions. It may also impact the valuation of defined benefit schemes or pensions in payment. Practitioners should be alert to this if they are dealing with a pension that is in payment due to ill health, for example if the pension member has been discharged from the armed forces on ill health grounds. The PODE may require this to be completed prior to undertaking their report, it would be sensible that this is sent to the client as soon as possible to avoid delays.

The key part of the PODE report, and often the most controversial, are the questions that the actuary is being asked to report on. The PAG report contains sample questions that can be asked of the PODE, subject to amendments for each case. The most common question to ask is how the pensions should be divided to equalise income in retirement. Whilst this may seem a straightforward request, as with anything in law, it can be more complex than it appears and could be open to interpretation. It is necessary to consider the date at which you are asking the PODE to work to for equalisation. This may be one party's state retirement date, the earliest date at which all pensions are in payment or another fixed date in the future. This is not set in stone as it varies from case to case. In some cases it may be more appropriate to look at equalising income when a particular pension comes into payment, for example an NHS pension that pays out at age 60, but for others it may be appropriate to equalise pensions when the parties are both at state retirement age. Instructions should be taken from a party on when they anticipate retiring, when their own pensions come into payment or when they envisage taking their pension credit.

If you are looking at a party's state retirement age, consider whose age you are using. By way of an example, consider a case where the first spouse has the smaller pension and is due to retire in 2030. The second spouse with the larger pension is not due to retire until 2035. If you ask the PODE to equalise income from the second spouse's state retirement age, then the calculation will equalise income at age 2035 and the percentage pension sharing order required will reflect that. However, the first spouse may start receiving their pension income from 2030. The pension will be in payment for 5 years longer than was anticipated when the PODE produced their figures which could result in less income being received. It is always important to check this, and if in doubt confirm the figures with a financial advisor or the PODE.

An alternative is to look at the earliest date that all pensions are in payment. This could result in the same situation arising if there is an age gap and the financially weaker party is younger. In these circumstances where there is an age gap or where agreement cannot be reached, it would be prudent to ask the PODE which date they consider to be the most appropriate to equalise pensions for their report, though the date used and the pension sharing order made is always a matter for the court. If there is a significant dispute between the parties, then a range of dates may be required from the PODE with the final decision left to the court to determine.

To ensure that inadvertent financial advice is not given by practitioners, engage with a financial advisor to consider this. assuming the PODE has been instructed as a single joint expert, their duty is to the court, if advice is required for the client, then this should be from a financial advisor. Alternatively, in a case that can afford it, look to instruct a shadow PODE to review the report and advise the client without the confines of being a single joint expert.

Public sector pensions add a further layer of complexity to matters. Different public sector schemes have different rules for when their pensions come into payment. Some examples include:

- Armed Forces Pension Scheme 2015 – state retirement age
- Armed Forces Pension Scheme 1975 - 60/65 (depending on service dates)
- NHS 2005 – age 60

It is important to consider this when looking at the equalisation date. If you are looking at equality of pension income, then equalising at a point in the future after the pension comes into payment for the pension member spouse, could result in an income gap. An income gap is the period where one party is in receipt of their pension, but the other has to wait before they can receive the income or choose to take it sooner but receive a reduced income to account for it being in payment for longer. This can occur in the uniformed services where a party could receive their pension immediately on retirement if they have completed a certain number of years' service, yet the non-member spouse in receipt of the pension sharing order may have to wait until a later age, such as 65 for the Armed Forces Pension Scheme 1975.

PAG 2 addresses this issue in Part 10 of PAG 2, which includes a number of proposals for how this can be addressed, including at Part 10 para 32:

- *a return to work by one or both parties;*
- *reverse pension sharing to create liquidity (though with tax consequences);*
- *maximising pension benefits by supplemental payments (including to State Pensions);*
- *deferring divorce;*
- *adjourning the application for a PSO;*
- *a deferred PSO;*
- *the pursuit of judicial separation (to preserve a spouse's pension if adjourning the application for a PSO);*
- *ongoing periodical payments paid from the pension in payment (contrary to the court's duty to achieve a clean break);*

- *a charge and/or security over other assets if adjourning the application for a PSO*

This is predominantly an issue in cases involving public sector pensions where the scheme's normal retirement date is pre-state retirement. In cases where the income gap is a real issue, a PODE can advise on what that gap is and potentially provide a capital figure for it. This may also be considered a loss of benefit that you would ask the court to consider under s.25(2)(h). There are many variables in these instances - it may be appropriate to seek a lump sum to meet the claim for a loss of benefit, or in cases where the equalisation date is after the pension member has retired (and of course, subject to the age of the non-member spouse at the time of the divorce), an earlier equalisation date may be appropriate to address this gap. The counter argument in these instances might be that the member-spouse will be unemployed, and their pension will be their income at that point, bearing in mind that without the benefit of a crystal ball neither party knows what the pension member will do when they leave their employment nor where their income will come from.

Further, a pension is an asset to meet income needs in retirement. It could be advanced that a non-member spouse with an income-generating career would be benefiting twice were they to equalise pensions based on a pre-state retirement age date, enjoying the benefit of a pension sharing order equalising at, say 55, whilst still having over 10 years of income generating employment head of them. In contrast, the pension member will be in receipt of a reduced income during this time, whilst the spouse doesn't receive any income from the pension sharing order. Both parties lose out in this instance.

These are complex issues and ones that often come down the individual facts of the case, there rarely being a clear right and wrong answer.

In cases where perhaps there is the potential for a periodical payments order order until retirement, it may be appropriate to equalise pensions from an earlier age so that the clean break can come into effect sooner. For example, pension income could be taken into consideration for mortgage calculations or to enable a party to afford a mortgage where their employment income alone may not enable that to happen. This may be appropriate in cases where the parties are near or over 55 and a mortgage over a reasonably short period of time, for example a ten-year mortgage to age 65, may be expensive. The additional pension income from a pension sharing order may assist in topping up their capital in the interim by way of a mortgage to meet their housing need. Mortgages aside, the pension income could be used to meet the financial weaker spouse's income needs prior to retirement age and negate a maintenance order.

There are cases where several age range calculations in a PODE report may be of use, though in practice this should be discouraged as the inevitable outcome is further dispute with each party seeking an order in the terms most favourable to them. Whilst the financial weaker spouse may be able to argue a need for a pension sharing order to equalise income from an earlier than usual age, consider the impact that the pension debit will have on the pension income of the member spouse. Will the reduced pension income enable them to meet their needs in their retirement? Or would the earlier equalisation reduce their pension to such an extent that they won't be able to live? A PODE report will include post-pension sharing income figures so that the effect on a pension sharing order can be seen for both the debit and credit members. This is of course a balancing act, and one of several factors to be considered when looking at the assets of a couple on divorce, whilst being mindful that pensions are often treated as a separate entity to pre-retirement income though of course there is a crossover in certain situations, as explained above.

A further reason for including multiple dates in the letter of instruction is to consider the treatment or pre- or post-separation pension accrual on divorce. This has become a contentious subject in the division of pensions on divorce since the *W v H* case of 2020 and are interlinked with other arguments about matrimonial and non-matrimonial property. The treatment of pension accrual outside of the period of marriage will be considered further below, but it is a reason to consider asking a PODE to undertake their calculations based on more than one date. When this is likely a feature of the case, the client should be prepared to provide dates of their employment and relevant promotions/salary increases during the marriage. A PODE may ask the relevant party to provide a history of their employment so that they can calculate the pension accrual over the relevant period, especially in defined benefit pension cases where pension accrual is based on salary, or cases where a pension is based on career average earnings, often referred to a CARE scheme. Pension contribution is not necessarily even over time, with pension contributions increasing in line with salary rises or increased service. It would also be sensible to forewarn your client of this so that they can begin to collate the necessary information in advance and avoid further delay.

The approach of the PODE will vary with some calculations being undertaken on a "straight line accrual" basis and some based on the salaries paid over the course of the pension-member's employment, which will require a significant amount of information about the member's employment history. For some public sector pensions based on salary, their pension accrual was a lot less in the early stages of their career (pre-marriage), and the greater increases in salary were later, during the marriage. A straight-line accrual assumes that the member earns their pension benefits evenly over time during their total career, which may benefit those seeking to ring-fence pre-marital pensions as it could increase the value of their pre-marital pensions which, when looking at pensions based on salary, assumes a greater pension was earned in the early stages of the career than actually was.

Not only is it dates of pensionable employment/service that should be provided in the letter of instruction, but also the dates of the relationship. It is not uncommon that disputes arise over which dates to use. For example, it is a regular occurrence that parties seek to argue that there was no or very limited period of cohabitation or even argue over when that cohabitation started or ended. The issue as to whether that is cohabitation or not is a judicial matter for determination by the court if not agreed, rather than a substantive argument to be had when drafting the letter of instruction.

One course of action may be to include each party's proposed dates in the letter of instruction, with the issue of when the parties did or did not cohabit left to the court and dealt with by way of statements and submissions at a hearing or perhaps as a discreet issue to be determined by arbitration, though this is not a preferred course of action as it increases the tension and animosity, as well as costs. Be mindful though that the more date ranges you are asking the PODE to consider, the more expensive the report is likely to be. If you are asking the PODE to consider a cohabitation start date that is a matter of months different than the other party's proposed date, consider whether it is cost effective to go down the road of further calculations and instead it may be sensible to elect the midpoint between the dates to avoid unnecessary costs. Obtaining a quote from the PODE may swiftly knock those arguments on the head and lead a party to adopt pragmatic and cost-effective way forward to avoid the unnecessary expense of multiple dates in the report.

It would be prudent to either agree dates being calculated at the FDA or if agreement cannot be reached, seek judicial input so that there is less scope for disagreement when drafting the letter of instruction.

When submitting the letter of instruction to the PODE, ensure that the relevant documents are enclosed at the earliest opportunity. Ensure that the CETVs of the pensions are enclosed, the relevant pages of the Form E and also the court order (if applicable) that sets out their instruction. If the costs of the report are being borne in unequal shares, ensure that the PODE is aware of that so that they can send separate invoices to each firm. If for any reason there is an unequal division of the costs or one party is paying for additional calculations, ensure this is confirmed in the court order and the letter of instruction.

Offsetting has previously been a popular means of treating pensions on divorce. Whether to consider offsetting or not depends on the circumstances of the case, in particular the asset base as a whole, the parties' needs, and the types of pensions involved. Significant case law has covered this issue and it will be further addressed below. However, it would be prudent to consider at an early stage whether offsetting may be an appropriate outcome in a case or something a party wishes to consider. Some PODE reports will include an offsetting figure as standard, whereas others will charge an additional fee for providing the relevant calculations. In limited asset cases where liquid capital to pay legal fees is not readily available, instruct a PODE that includes an offsetting figure as standard. In all cases where offsetting is being considered, ask the

PODE in the letter of instruction to consider it. If you are considering offsetting pension assets for capital in a property, identify this in the letter of instruction and set out the agreed equity in the property so that the PODE knows what figure they are working with. It may avoid a later question from the expert, incurring further expense for the parties in agreeing a figure and providing the information to the PODE. As mentioned previously, time is often of the essence when it comes to a PODE report, so the more information provided in the initial instruction the better.

The PAG report contains a comprehensive template draft letter of instruction which is intended to be used in the majority of cases. Familiarising yourself with this letter would be a sensible exercise, remembering that it has been drafted by experienced and highly respected professionals from both legal, financial and actuarial fields, and creates a sensible basis for letters of instruction. In addition, the more standardised the letter of instruction across the legal profession, the less time and cost incurred in agreeing a draft before, during or after an FDA which will be a benefit for all concerned. That said, the letter should be tailored to the individual facts of the case, rather than sent without amendment which could ask irrelevant questions or result in a more complex report than is required. The draft letter of instruction in the PAG report is a guide and a template to be amended by practitioners. When considering the use of the template letter of instruction and the questions contained therein, in particular the question to calculate equalisation of both capital and income, HHJ Hess noted in *SP v AL* that *"it should be remembered that these are options provided in the specimen letter and it is not necessary for both of them need to be included in the actual letter"*. The letter of instruction should be amended to meet the needs of the case in hand and not blindly followed without due consideration of the information required.

CHAPTER FIVE

OFFSETTING AND RINGFENCING PRE/ POST-MARITAL PENSIONS

Offsetting pensions, the practice of one-party retaining pension assets in lieu of other capital has long been considered a reasonable outcome in financial remedy proceedings and has frequently been an outcome in cases. It has been such a dominant practice in this area that PAG 2 refers to it as "*offsetting: the dominant practice*".

Money in a pension pot is not the same as money in, for example, a property. The phrase most commonly used in the context of offsetting is that it is like comparing apples and pears. They are not the same and it is incorrect to consider them as similar. Historically it was not uncommon for pension assets to be considered alongside other capital assets, however the case of *Martin-Dye v Martin-Dye [2006] 4 All ER 779* brought about a change in approach to the matter.

By way of background, the matter was determined by a District Judge who found that a 57/43% split in assets in favour of the wife was a fair outcome. Neither party objected to the asset split, however the appeal was based on the Judge including pension assets in the total capital pot, with the wife retaining more of the non-pension assets to offset the husband retaining his larger pension. The husband was left with less liquid capital and instead a greater income source. The pensions in questions were in payment, which the Court of Appeal held required them to be treated differently than capital assets. Thorpe LJ stated at para 61 that:

> *"They are to be characterised as 'other financial resources' within the s 25(2)(a) classification. For they do not sit comfortably in the category of 'property', since they are unrealisable and non-transferable. Nor do they sit comfortably in the category of 'income' because, although purely an income stream, the income does not derive from future endeavour but from past employment or contribution which will generally have been effected during the years of marriage."*

This paragraph clearly set out that pensions are not necessarily to be treated the same as other capital assets. It is worth noting though that this was a time pre-pension freedoms which have since enabled a party to liquidate their pension funds and was also in the context of pensions in payment rather than a pension that has not yet come into payment.

Martin-Dye concluded that in that particular instant, it was preferable for pensions to be treated separately from the capital asset and shared by way of a pension sharing order. The percentage split of the total pensions in the case was in identical terms to the capital split, rather than by having regard to the income it generated, an approach that now would be considered incorrect and one that practitioners would shy away from. This case provided the authority that pension sharing orders are the preferred way forward when dealing with pensions in payment, rather than offsetting for other non-pension assets.

The court has tried many times and in various cases to look at offsetting, as have academics and barristers. Rhys Taylor and Hilary Woodward published an article in 2015 entitled *"Apples or Pears? Pension offsetting on divorce"* which was published in Family Law [2012] vol. 42 page 1234 and subsequently quoted by HHJ Lord

Meston QC in his judgement in the case of *WS v WS [2015] EWHC 3941 (Fam)* at para 56. The article is summarised by the Judge, noting the difficulties in obtaining a *"one size fits all"* offsetting figure for use in financial remedy cases. The article details how they gave 3 scenarios to 14 different PODEs, the outcome being a variety of different proposed offsetting figures that at times varied hugely. Taylor and Woodward noted that "*the range of assumptions, even with the imperfections of this exercise, are arresting nevertheless*", highlighting the difficulties in obtaining an offsetting figure that is universally accepted, an issue that is still prevalent now.

The judgement of HHJ Lord Meston QC succinctly sets out the changing approach of the court to pensions on divorce, and offsetting, summarising at paragraphs 52 – 54 a brief summary of the cases that had considered offsetting to that point and notes that "*It is quite apparent when looking again at the rival arguments and different figures suggested that there is no obviously right figure or correct calculation*". This remains the case and part of the difficulty with offsetting is that there is no agreed way to calculate the appropriate offsetting figure, by way of example there are differing discounts for "utility" taken into account, which is covered below. In that particular case, the court found that using a capital figure based on the Duxbury tables to be appropriate in the case, though it is noteworthy that the court highlighted that it was not being asked to capitalise periodical payments and was instead being asked to capitalise a guaranteed pension income (para 65). It would seem strange to practitioners now, a short number of years on from this case, that an expert report was not sanctioned by the court. One would hope that were an application for a PODE put before the court now, on identical facts, a PODE report would be ordered at the earliest opportunity.

Much discussion about offsetting and how to calculate the correct offsetting figure has followed from cases involving defined benefit pension scheme, such as public sector pensions. The PAG 2 guide, at Part 7, has a detailed consideration of the issue of offsetting and the use of CETVs as a figure for basing an offsetting calculation. PAG 2 cautions practitioners on the risks of using the CETV for offsetting, highlighting that it is not always appropriate nor an accurate figure to use in the circumstances of a case. Caution should be exercised here, it being noted in the report (para 7.4) that "*Where there have been claims of negligence made against family lawyers in the field of pensions, it has overwhelmingly been in cases where offsetting has been the chosen remedy, not pension sharing*". PAG 2 does, however, note that " *If the case solely involves Defined Contribution funds, which have no guarantees, then the CE may be a good starting point for valuation for offsetting*". Nevertheless, if in doubt, a PODE should be instructed to properly consider the offsetting calculation.

The complexities that require PODE input often arises in cases involving defined benefit schemes, though not exclusively. In some defined contribution cases it not appropriate to simply rely on the CETV. In cases involving defined benefit pensions, there has been much made of the accuracy or using the CETV as the basis for valuing the pension benefits. The PAG 2 guide notes that a CETV of a defined benefit pension is often not a reliable value for divorce purposes and recommends the instruction of a PODE to properly consider the value of the pension benefits attributable to the member. This is also known as the "fair actuarial value", or "market consistent capital value". A PODE will be able to calculate what they consider to be a FAV for the pension in question, addressing claims from non-member spouses that a pension has been "undervalued".

In cases where there is a defined benefit pension, it is almost always prudent to instruct a PODE to properly consider the position, whether the parties are looking to consider pension capital values or pension income in retirement. The methods used by PODEs in calculating pension values for offsetting is a complex area and set out in more detail by the authors of the PAG 2report, which highlights that there are different methods of calculating the offsetting figure. For practitioners, as a general rule, if a party wishes to offset capital assets for pension assets where they include defined benefit schemes, the instruction of a PODE should be at the forefront of everyone's minds in particular to avoid potential negligence claims in the future should the calculations not be done correctly.

In the circumstances of a case where a single joint expert has been instructed, particularly in low to medium value cases where other assets are limited, this does put a party in a difficult position if they are unhappy with the outcome of the report. In those circumstances, the starting point ought to be to ask the expert for clarification which may shed some light on the figures and help alleviate the concerns of a client, before looking at a second opinion. Ultimately, in contested proceedings, it is a matter for the court as to how to handle an offsetting scenario and what figure to use to offset pension assets for other capital assets. Outside of the formal court arena, it becomes a decision for the parties as to on what terms they resolve the division of the matrimonial assets though it would always be wise to ensure that offsetting calculations are prepared by a PODE and not lawyers.

In cases that are being resolved using non-court dispute resolution, the involvement of a financial neutral may assist the parties in understanding the report, with an independent financial advisor being asked to help the parties and the practitioner interpret the report.

Offsetting has been reconsidered by the High Court in the landmark case of W v H [2020]. HHJ Hess considered a case of modest means, save for the pension assets, rather than the oft-cited high net worth cases reported. This was a case that would be described as a "needs" case. The pensions in the case included the husband's defined benefit pension scheme with a value of £2,155,475 and a defined contribution plan with a CETV of £58,653. The wife had a defined benefit scheme with a CETV of £138,939 and a defined contribution plan with a CETV of £13,798. The parties began living together in 1999, marrying in 2005 and separating in 2016. It is key that the husband contributed to his pension prior to their marriage, having been with his employer since 1987.

HHJ Hess, when considering the matter of pensions, set out the 3 questions that he felt had to be determined. The first being whether pensions should be divided based on income or capital equality, the second whether pre-marital pension contributions should be excluded and the third whether the court should separate pension assets from other capital assets or group them together and undertaken an offsetting exercise. These were important questions that needed to be addressed. There have been changes since the earlier pension cases mentioned above, such as the more widespread use of CETVs, the pension freedoms that enable a member spouse to essentially "cash in" their pension and release the capital, and of course the PAG report.

This case was a milestone in considering the treatment of pensions on divorce in the context of the first PAG guide and has been cited by lawyers in correspondence/submissions where pre-marital pension contributions are a feature. HHJ Hess gave a ringing endorsement to the PAG report, stating (para 59) that the report should *"be treated as being prima facie persuasive in the areas it has analysed, although of course susceptible to judicial oversight and criticism"*. The PAG report is not a binding authority, but clearly the indication from HHJ Hess is that this is a report that should have significant weight attached to it, which is likely going to result in practitioners being expected to follow its terms closely. That does not prevent practitioners form making representations that are contrary to the broad principles in the PAG report, though it may be described as an uphill struggle for them in light of this case.

As to the issue of income vs capital, this was considered in the PAG report which noted that predominantly the parties' needs would dictate that focussing on income is the most appropriate way in which to equalise the parties' pensions. A pension is an income generating asset, and though there are certain circumstances where it is appropriate to focus on equalising capital, in needs cases it is likely to require an income-based assessment to achieve an outcome that is fair to the parties. The PAG 2 report set this out at para 6.13 with reasons for that view, which include noting that *"a division that pays little or no attention to income-yield may have the effect of reducing the standard of living of the less well-off party significantly."* No party wishes to give up more of their pension than they need to, and certainly no party wants a lower standard of living in retirement than they need to either, so it is important that proper expert input is obtained to ensure that this does not happen and to mitigate any potential claims against legal advisors arising from inappropriate pension sharing orders.

There are of course cases where it is unnecessary to instruct a PODE to consider incomes in retirement, and instead a division based on CETVs would be more appropriate. As a starting point, if the pension assets are standard defined contribution pension schemes, then a PODE report may incur unnecessary expense and delay. Where the total values of the pensions are less than £100,000, the PAG 2 guide authors do not consider that a PODE report is necessary (para 6.10). In addition, younger parties who are not facing retirement soon, those who have limited pension assets or cases involving a very short marriage may not require a PODE report and the costs of obtaining a report may outweigh the assets involved. As set out previously, proportionality is important, as are legal fees, and this must be remembered when advising a client. Beware though, this is not an exhaustive list and expert advice should be sought before advising a client that a report is not necessary.

One key exclusion is cases involving uniformed public services such as the armed forces, the unique nature of those schemes will invariably require PODE input. In W v H, HHJ Hess found that given the nature of the pension assets, especially the husband's significant defined benefit pension, together with their ages, meant that income should be the driving factor over capital. This has now become the dominant approach in cases involving defined benefit pensions and has received positive judicial treatment post- W v H.

By focussing on the income that is produced rather than the capital value, this segregates the pension assets from the other capital assets in contrast to earlier judgements on this issue. By doing so, and treating the pensions separately, the issue of needs arises more so as the other capital is not considered to meet post-retirement needs as much as perhaps it was previously. This impacts arguments of ring-fencing, as the husband in this instance discovered.

The husband sought to ring fence the part of his pension that was accrued prior to the relationship based on dividing the pension by the number of years over which he has contributed to it, then multiplying it by the number of years of the relationship. This is known as a straight-line calculation, as set out above, and has been a common means of calculating pension accrual, usually for offsetting purposes, but is not necessarily correct. HHJ Hess refers to this and notes that this carries a significant risk of unfairness (para 61.(i)). This would achieve an unfair result in cases of defined benefit pensions where the value of the pension is linked to the member's salary, as HHJ Hess sets out in para 61.(vii) of his judgement. In these instances, and matters involving uniformed services, a significant proportion of the pension may have accrued during the marriage, which won't be reflected in a straight calculation of marital accrual as the early stages of a career would have resulted in limited pension accrual, increasing more so as the member's career progressed and during the marriage, especially where the pension is based on the final salary. This of course is also the issue in cases where the parties have separated and not resolved their finances. A party may have continued to work, accruing pension rights and in turn increasing the value of that pension post-separation. If proceedings are initiated many years after separation, the CETV provided will be reflective of those post-separation endeavours and it becomes a ring-fencing argument. For those parties who do not feel that it is necessary to have a financial order on divorce, they ought to be reminded of this. In these types of cases, the input of a PODE will be necessary to establish how much of the pension was accrued during the marriage.

W v H also identified that this approach to ring fencing pre-marital pension accrual is akin to arguing that the ring-fenced pension is non-matrimonial property. That of course brings into the equation the separate legal principles that apply to matrimonial and non-matrimonial property, and the relevant case law that applies to it. It leads to discussion of needs, mingling and fairness. Fairness and needs are of course at the forefront of the court's mind when considering the division of the matrimonial assets. HHJ Hess refers to *White v White [2000] UKHL 54, Miller v Miller; McFarlane v McFarlane [2006] UKHL 24 and JL v SL [2015] EWHC 360* in his judgement, noting that "*fairness and equality usually ride hand in hand*". As to mingling, in these matters it is rare for pension assets to be mingled, unlike cash assets or cash contributions to the former matrimonial home given the nature of the asset, though it may be possible for one party's capital to be invested in a pension in the other party's name for a variety of reasons, with the mingling of assets not being a problem until they come to attempt to unravel it on divorce. It is a long-established principle that in a needs case the court can have recourse to any asset, matrimonial or non-matrimonial in order to meet a party's needs. The PAG report at para 4.2 makes a sweeping statement that the majority of cases, even those with values of millions, are considered "needs" cases. This is affirmed by HHJ Hess at para 61.(iv) where he goes as far as to say that he there is little justification for excluding any part of the pension on the basis of it being non-matrimonial unless the income produced by the pensions exceeds a party's needs in retirement. He further explains it is unlikely that many pensions will have a value of such a level as to take them over the "needs" threshold and into the arena of sharing instead. As such, the inference is that it is only in exceptional cases that ring-fencing pre or post marital pension accrual will achieve a fair outcome.

However, each case rests on its facts and there may be circumstances where it is appropriate for there to be at least consideration given to ring fencing pension accrual that occurred outside the marriage. In cases of defined benefit schemes, where a simply straight-line calculation is not appropriate, it may be prudent to ask the actuary to undertake calculations on both marital accrual and total accrual in order to establish what income is likely to be achieved from excluding some of the pensions. This will likely incur a cost as it is an additional calculation, but that should be confirmed by the PODE. The court may order at the FDA that a number of dates are considered so that the FDR judge has all the information before them to give an informed indication on that point, in particular, whether the income from marital accrual only will be sufficient to meet a party's needs in retirement. This has to be considered in the context of s.25 MCA 1973 which requires the court to consider this issue in the context of the parties age and the duration of the marriage. Would it be fair for a short childless marriage of, for example, 5 years with a couple in their mid-30's to result in a pension sharing order of the entire pension where one party had 10 year's pre-marital public sector pension contribution? To put it differently, is it fair that a party in their mid-30s with another 30+ years' of work ahead be able to share in the entire pension rather than just marital accrual? Does that party really have a need for pension income in retirement when they have over 30 years to accrue their own pension? These are of course submission points for a hearing or for discussion in mediation/non-court dispute resolution, but it would not harm either the parties or the court to have this information from a PODE to assist, and guidance sought at an FDR. Ultimately if an agreement cannot be reached then the court will have to determine the matter.

The final question addressed in W v H was the issue of offsetting. In limited asset cases it may not be possible or appropriate to offset a pension sharing order for capital, it may result in one party leaving the marriage with no liquid capital with which to meet their immediate capital needs such as a house deposit. HHJ Hess also refers to the PAG guide in para 62.(i) and reiterates their view, which in turn reiterates the "orthodox" view of Thorpe LJ in Martin-Dyer v Martin-Dyer, that pension assets should be treated as a distinct asset from other capital and not offset against other assets. HHJ Hess warns against this approach, citing potential unfairness if the calculations are not done correctly. The example given is the unfairness that may arise from one party retaining assets they cannot realise, whilst the other retains cash or other liquid assets that can be used to meet immediate needs.

By way of an example, if a 40-year-old retains their pension in lieu of the equity in the FMH, they cannot access the money in their pension until they are 55, though that age is shortly due to rise. Even then, releasing money from their pension may involve punitive tax consequences depending on the sums involved. The W v H approach is to avoid offsetting pension assets and instead consider pensions as a standalone asset separate to capital. This has been re-affirmed in subsequent case law and PAG 2

This leads on the discussion of "utility" and the discount that should be applied to a pension valuation to reflect that one party has the benefit of that cash asset immediately whereas the party with the pension has to wait to access the benefit of the pension asset. This has been referred to in case law and the PAG 2 guide (para 7.37 onwards), though the PAG guide is clear that this should not be a matter for a PODE and instead is a matter for the court to consider when exercising the discretionary criteria in s.25 MCA 1973. There is no hard and fast rule for this (para 7.40) though they do provide guidance to consider when looking at this in more detail.

It appears from W v H that the outcome on the question of offsetting is that it is likely to now become rarer as a result of that judgement. The case clearly sets out that pensions should be treated in isolation from the other capital assets, and offsetting runs contrary to that. For those with healthy pensions who wish to retain them, it would appear that they are going to have more of a struggle now than they would perhaps have done previously. This is not an absolute bar to offsetting, but a clear judicial indication that it is not presently the favoured approach on divorce.

A serious consideration with offsetting is that one party may end up capial rich but income poor. It may well be the desired outcome for one party to retain the family home, but when they reach retirement, they may find themselves with limited income. That could cause difficulties servicing outgoings and necessitate downsizing. These longer-term issues are often overlooked by the parties to a divorce who are focussed instead on the here and now. It is important that this is considered and discussed with a financial advisor who can undertake a cash flow projection exercise to look at how long the available capital will last before it begins to run out.

The court is very aware of pension assets and are likely to question the absence of a pension sharing order where a D81 shows a significant disparity in the parties' pension positions.

In those cases, it is suggested by the PAG guide that may be sensible to explain the rationale behind the order in both the D81 but also as a recital to the order. Cases where the parties have agreed offsetting but not explained this to the court could find themselves having to answer questions from the court on the fairness of the agreement, which may trigger one party to try and resile from it or seek to suggest that the court has rejected the order, thereafter, seeking a share of the pension in addition to the capital they have retained through their agreement to offset. Whilst in theory this does not sound fair and may seem far-fetched, it is a potential problem and one that practitioners should be aware of. In the event that the court rejects an order, or raises a query on it and a party resiles from it, issuing Form A may be appropriate with the court asked to deal with the existing agreement as a discreet issue prior to the matter proceeding in the usual way, or arbitration could be considered to resolve the matter. The Form E can be used to explain the background to the matter, following *Xydhias* the agreement loses any without prejudice privilege it had and should be annexed to the Form E with the other supporting documents to demonstrate that an agreement had been reached. At the FDA, seek a direction that the parties file statements detailing their rationale behind the agreement and setting out why they either think it fair or no longer wish to be bound by it. The court should then be asked to list a hearing to determine that issue the outcome either being the consent order upheld or the consent order being rejected and the matter proceeding to an FDA/FDR.

As previously stated, each case rests on its own facts, but the decision of HHJ Hess is likely to have significant consequences for anyone who wishes to ring fence their pension contributions accrued outside the marriage. The *W v H* case also involved a large pension and parties who were aged 48 and 50 at the time of the hearing and had a long marriage. Cases involving younger parties with smaller pensions may find that offsetting is an attractive proposal and a suitable outcome, such as cases with lower value CETVs (less than £100,000 total) all in defined contribution schemes. Consider also that in certain cases with small pensions, the cost of implementing a pension sharing order can be expensive and it may be more appropriate to look at offsetting instead of sharing the pension if the costs of doing so outweighs the benefit to the party. This should be approached with caution and appropriate advice sought from a PODE if in doubt. Many PODEs will offer the service of reporting only on offsetting calculations, so if it is a case with a small defined benefit pension and one that attracts high implementation fees, such as Teachers' Pensions which charges £3,250 to implement a pension sharing order, it may be sensible to instruct a PODE to provide only offsetting. The fee for this is potentially less than a full report on pension sharing.

The outcome of *W v H* may now lead practitioners in negotiations, and the court in contested proceedings, to separate pension assets from the other capital assets more so than they did before. Offsetting pensions is likely to be seen as less than favourable moving forward than it has historically been. The outcome of this case is clear in that respect, and practitioners should be alert to the need to instruct a PODE in the appropriate cases to ensure that the correct calculations are carried out, practitioners should not be calculating the pension sharing percentages themselves where you are looking at an income equalisation case or offsetting involving defined benefit pensions.

The case of W v H was revisited by HHJ Hess in the case of SP v AL[2024] EWFC 72 (B). Attention is drawn in particular to paragraphs 34 onwards where HHJ Hess reiterated the earlier dicta of W v H, but expands on this in light of PAG 2.

Not only did HHJ Hess reaffirm the earlier position of Martin-Dye that pensions should, if possible be treated independently of other assets, but he also addressed 2 issues of importance. The first was the question of capital vs income equalisation and the second was the issue of whether pre-marital pensions should be ring fenced and protected from division.

Turning to the first question, as set out in PAG and PAG2, in cases involving defined benefit schemes the proper focus should be on a division of the pension asset based on the income that it generates. In coming to this conclusion, HHJ Hess reiterated the relevant paragraphs of PAG 2 and highlights that the CETV is not always the most appropriate measure of the value of the pension asset, in particular where there is an age gap and where the pensions defined benefit. There is a further observation on the use of the precedent letter of instruction with a cautious from Hess not to rely on it as drafted, as referred to above.

In respect of the ring fencing of pre-marital pensions, this issue was again addressed by HHJ Hess. At the time of W v H, as set out above, the approach was that in needs cases, with PAG commenting that needs cases could still involve pensions values in the "low millions", any attempts to ring-fence pre-marital pensions would likely fail. PAG 2 considered this, and the approach taken in the guide was that whilst needs will need to be met, as is well established, needs is one of the factors in s.25 and the court must have regard to the other s.25 factors to come to an outcome that is said.

One point considered in PAG 2 was short cohabitation/marriages and a pension need. PAG 2 sets out at para 4.11 "*Short cohabitation/marriage cases may require consideration of whether any asserted need for retirement income is a 'relationship generated' need to justify invasion of an otherwise non matrimonial asset. The requirement of a nexus between the relationship and a financial need to be met by a matrimonial claim has long been recognised by the case law*". In those cases where there is a retirement income need and the duration of the relationship is short, practitioners should consider whether the income need is relationship generated or not. In those cases where the income need is not relationship generated; it could be suggested that an invasion of the non-matrimonial element of a pension should be considered when looking at the division of the pension on divorce.

Relationship length was considered by HHJ Hess in SP v AL, observing that the duration of the marriage is not from the moment the couple say "I do", rather it is to include pre-marital cohabitation where there has been a seamless transition from cohabitation of marriage. There is established case law, as set out at para 14 which deals with the question of cohabitation. HHJ Hess quotes VV v VV EWFC 41 stating:

> "*The origin of the cohabitation jurisprudence (so far as relevant to the sharing principle) lies in the decision of Deputy High Court Judge Nicholas Mostyn QC (as he then was) in GW v RW [2003] EWHC 611 at para 33 where he said: 'Thus in my judgment where a relationship moves seamlessly from cohabitation to marriage without any major alteration in the way the couple live, it is unreal and artificial to treat the periods differently.' Those dicta have stood the test of time*"

Para 40 is a key paragraph that practitioners should familiar themselves with. HHJ Hess reiterated the relevant paragraphs of the PAG 2 report and sets out that the court must have regard to the s.25 factors and:

> "*Thus, the court will have regard to the length of seamless cohabitation/marriage when determining the extent to which it is fair and reasonable to divide the 'non-matrimonial' element of any capital or any pension. All cases will be determined upon their own facts. The 'marital' element of any pension will usually be shared equally. For the reasons set out above, in needs-based cases, the timing and source of the pension saving is not necessarily relevant, but the Court will nevertheless have regard to the length (or shortness) of the seamless cohabitation/marriage in determining the extent to which the needs of the claiming party will justify a division of the pre-cohabitation/*

> *marriage element of the pension... The requirement of a nexus between the relationship and a financial need to be met by a matrimonial claim has long been recognised by the case law*"

In those cases where there are healthy pension pots, and those cases where there is sufficient income to meet needs, the jurisprudence from SP v AL shows that a departure from equality to reflect the pre-marital pension is a more feasible outcome than it was only a short time ago. It is well established case law that needs must be met, but there will be cases where the pension assets are particularly large in the context of the other assets of the marriage, such as those with lengthy service in the public sector and limited capital. In those instances, it is entirely possible that the income needs of the parties in their retirement can be met whilst still recognising the pre-marital contribution made by one party.

With the advent of PAG 2 and its endorsement by the court, there is a much clearer picture for practitioners now, which is that attempts to disregard lengthy periods of cohabitation prior to the marriage are unlikely to be successful. PAG 2 highlighted this and it was referred to through that report that the date for establishing "marital" contributions should include pre-marital contribution. Issues over the length of cohabitation are a matter to be addressed by the parties ideally prior to the instruction of a PODE. If this is not possible, as was the case here, having 2 sets of calculations undertaken to provide both, with the court ultimately deciding or the parties reaching an agreement without judicial involvement and the proper pension sharing figure being identified thereafter from the report.

Any discussion on needs, ring-fencing, and the treatment of non-matrimonial pensions—particularly those accrued pre-marriage—

must now be framed in light of the Supreme Court's decision in Standish v Standish [2025] UKSC 26. Although the case did not directly refer to pensions, its clarification of the sharing principle and the concept of matrimonialisation (a new term introduced in this case) could have ramifications for how pensions are treated.

In *Standish*, the Supreme Court considered whether assets transferred between spouses during the marriage remained non-matrimonial or had become matrimonial assets. At paragraph 49, the Court stated that *"the sharing principle only applies to matrimonial property and does not apply to non-matrimonial property."*

For practitioners, this allows submissions that certain pension assets, particularly those accrued before the marriage, should be treated as non-matrimonial and therefore excluded from equal division.

However, the Court also reiterated that needs remain a paramount consideration. Non-matrimonial pensions can still be shared if required to meet the financial needs of the non-member spouse. This means that while Standish strengthens the case for ring-fencing pre-marital pensions, it does not create an prevent the court from calling on that pre-marital asset where it is required to meet needs, and the court retains discretion to call upon non-matrimonial property in those circumstances.

PAG 2 also noted the recent introduction of the Galbraith Tables as a means of providing an indication of the offsetting value of pensions . They provide an early indication of the offsetting value and re a useful aid when considering the instruction of a PODE. At a Glance 2025 - 2026 notes that *"The tables are likely to be of use in those many cases where the cost of expert reporting is disproportionate to the issues at large."* In low-value cases the use of the Galbraith Tables may assist in helping consider the issue of offsetting and provided the parties with at least a ballpark figure for calculating the capital sum that could be paid in lieu of a pension sharing order. The tables are a guide and a useful tool to assist those considering offsetting pensions. For those who wish to protect their pre-marital pension contributions, especially those who may have started contributing to a public sector pension at an early age, the execution of a pre-nuptial agreement may be the most effective means of protecting the non-matrimonial element of their pension. The law on these agreements is beyond the scope of this book, but entering into one of these agreements would be a sensible precaution for many.

CHAPTER SIX

UNIFORMED SERVICES AND PUBLIC SECTOR PENSIONS

A review of the PAG report will note that the exemptions to their recommendations in respect of the treatment of pensions on divorce will often follow with a caveat excluding uniformed services pensions. These pensions include the Armed Forces Pension Schemes ("AFPS") and these predominantly involve one of 3 pension schemes – AFPS 1975, AFPS 2005 and AFPS 2015. There are other pension schemes such as those that are accrued by reservists which may also come up in divorce cases, and those have their own rules. The AFPS pensions are referred to as unfunded public sector pensions, members do not pay pension contributions directly from their salary and each pension scheme has different rules on when the pension comes into payment, when it is paid in retirement, lump sums, commutation and accrual rate. These pensions are not straightforward and the input of a PODE is almost certainly required when one of these schemes is present.

The AFPS 1975 pension was in place until 5 April 2005 when it closed to new members. Prior to that, anyone who joined one of the armed forces and was over the age of 18 (ranks) or 21 (officers) began accruing pension right under the AFPS 1975 scheme. New entrants to the armed forces after 5 April 2005 were not eligible to become members of that scheme and instead were enrolled in the 2005 scheme. Existing service personnel continued to remain members of the 1975 scheme and continued to accrue pension benefits in that scheme, though were given the choice of transferring their benefits to the 2005 scheme if they wanted to.

From 1 April 2015, all members of the armed forces were enrolled in the 2015 scheme save for a certain group of service personnel who were not required to be enrolled in the 2015 scheme due to their age. This led to the McCloud case, which will be addressed further below, whereby it was found that the government had acted illegally in providing this transitional protection as it was discrimination based on age.

The 1975 scheme includes an automatic lump sum when the service member retires of 3x the annual pension income. This is tax free and is payable on retirement, provided they have passed their immediate pension point. A member reaches their immediate pension point if they are under 55 and have completed 16 years' service as an officer or 22 years' service in other ranks or are over the age of 55. For members who leave before 55 but have passed their immediate pension point, a fixed pension income is paid to age 55 and thereafter it increases to take account of the rise in cost of living since their leaving the forces and thereafter in line with CPI. If a service member leaves the armed forces prior to their immediate pension point they are known as deferred members. They will receive their pension income when they reach the deferred pension age of either 60 or 65. Pension accrued due to service prior to April 2006 is paid at 60, service after April 2006 is paid at 65. This means that there may be circumstances where a deferred pension is paid in increments, the first lump sum and pension income from 60 and a further lump sum and increased income from 65. Pension paid is based on rank and salary at the time of leaving the service and is a defined benefit scheme. This is one of the AFPS pension schemes referred to a "legacy scheme" in the context of McCloud.

The AFPS 2005 scheme was introduced in April 2005. From then, all new members of the armed forces were enrolled into that scheme. The scheme is a final salary defined benefit scheme, which also pays out a lump sum of 3x the annual pension income on the member's retirement. The AFPS 2005 pension gives members the opportunity to surrender part of their lump sum in exchange for a greater pension income, known as "inverse commutation". This will reduce the lump sum that is paid out but increase the pension income. The immediate pension point for the 2005 scheme is age 55, there is not the same option as in the 1975 scheme to receive your pension if you have completed a minimum period of service prior to age 55.

However, the 2005 scheme introduced an Early Departure Payment (EDP) which is payable if the pension member is over 40 but under 55 and has completed 18 years' service as a regular member of the armed forces. This is a feature unique to the armed forces. The EDP is made up of both a lump sum and also a regular income, the income ceasing when the member reaches the deferred retirement age and receives their pension instead. The lump sum is 3x the annual deferred pension and is tax free. EDP is not a pension, and it is not capable of being shared. This is an important point to be aware of, and it is crucial that when discussing pension income with a pension member you should identify whether it is their pension or EDP they are in receipt of. A CETV will confirm this if in doubt. When considering EDP income, as it is not a pension it cannot be shared by way of a pension sharing order. When instructing a PODE not only should you consider whether EDP is being included in the calculations, it could be excluded in the letter of instruction, but also ensure that the report is reviewed carefully once received so that the treatment of the EDP income is properly understood. If a PODE report is being obtained and the expert is asked to equalise income at a date prior to the scheme's normal deferred pension age, the only income may be EDP income. In that instance the PODE may consider the EDP income as if it were pension income and equalise incomes accordingly. It is crucial that the inclusion of EDP income is considered when instructing a PODE. Further, when considering the income gap/loss of benefit point above, EDP could be included in that figure despite it not being a pension itself.

PAG 2 addressed this point (I.25) and clearly recommend that despite not being a pension, they should be taken into account when considering the division of pensions on divorce.

Members of both the AFPS 1975 and AFPS 2005 pensions who were in service in 2015 were automatically enrolled in the AFPS 2015 scheme. Their rights under these legacy schemes remained in situ pending their retirement, but their continued service accrued pension rights under the 2015 scheme. When the member is in a position to take their pension, the pension that is paid under the 1975 and 2005 final salary schemes is based on the rank and salary at the point of leaving the armed forces, not based on the rank and salary when these schemes closed in 2015.

The most recent incarnation of the AFPS pension is the 2015 scheme. This has proven to be a controversial scheme as this, along with similar schemes affecting other public sector employees such as Police, Fire, civil service and the NHS, has resulted in the McCloud judgement. The AFPS 2015 pension is a Career Average Revalued Earnings scheme, known as a CARE scheme. Instead of being linked to the pension member's final salary at the time of retirement as AFPS 1975 and 2005 are, it is based on the members average salary over their time in the armed forces. The AFPS 2015 pension immediate pension point is aged 60, instead of age 55 for the 2005 scheme. If a member is still serving at age 60 then they will be entitled to take their pension immediately upon leaving the armed forces.

Similar to the 2005 scheme, the AFPS 2015 pension scheme also includes EDP as a feature of it. With the 2015 scheme a member is entitled to EDP after they attain the age of 40 and if they have completed 20 years' service, in contrast to the 18 under the 2005 scheme. The EDP is 2.25x the member's annual deferred pension rather than the 3x under the 2005 scheme. A 2015 scheme member can choose to give up their EDP lump sum to increase their EDP income, however if this is being considered in the context of a divorce then financial advice should be sought. As this is an EDP payment, it is not a benefit that a spouse will also have as the beneficiary of a pension sharing order as the EDP cannot be shared, as mentioned above.

There is no automatic lump sum with the 2015 scheme. However, the 2015 pension provides members with the option to exchange some of their pension income for a lump sum, which does have the effect of reducing the pension income that will be paid. This is commutation.

In the context of a divorce, it is essential that this is borne in mind if the pension member is due to imminently retire and pension income in retirement is an important feature. It would be possible for a pension member to commute their pension to generate a greater lump sum and thereby reduce their pension income with a view to trying to frustrate their spouse's pension sharing order claims. If acting for the non-service member and the service member is due to retire imminently, it would be prudent to seek an undertaking that the pension is not commuted to preserve the pension income and request updating disclosure after receipt of the lump sum to confirm the destination of the funds. A member has to elect to commute part of their pension and it may be appropriate to ask for copies of all correspondence from Veterans UK relating to their impending retirement to ensure that the non-member spouse has a full appreciation of what income and/or capital is being received by their former spouse. Whilst there is a duty of ongoing financial disclosure, these are not documents that a party or practitioner may automatically think to request or provide copies of.

As to lump sums generally, it would be possible and arguably a sensible exercise to request that a percentage of the lump sum is paid to solicitors to be held to joint order pending the proceedings being concluded. If the necessary criteria for a s.37 MCA 1973 is satisfied and there is a real risk that the lump sum could be dissipated or removed from the jurisdiction, a court application may be required to preserve the capital. Applications of this nature should be treated with caution, a misjudged application where the court is not satisfied that the necessary criteria are met, could result in a costs order being made. A thorough review of the s.37 criteria and associated case law would be wise before an application of this order is made. The court could legitimately take the approach that in the absence of a specific risk that the lump sum will be dissipated, the use of the money will come out in the disclosure process and if necessary, an add back argument may be run at a final hearing if there are dissipation issues.

A CETV for the AFPS pension schemes should be applied for by the service member, or Form P sent to Veterans UK, at an early stage in proceedings. Veterans UK will provide a free CETV once per year, though for some members still serving and who have passed their immediate pension point there will be no value attributed to the pension on the basis that it would be payable immediately, yet on payment of a fee a CETV can be provided. In addition, the service member's dates for service will also not be provided with a free CETV. If there are likely to be discussions about ring fencing pensions based on pre-marital accrual, the paid for CETV will provide the necessary dates for pension accrual that are required for the PODE letter of instruction. AFPS members are also sent an annual benefits statement and have access through their intranet system to obtain a valuation of their benefits. It is not uncommon for this to be provided to solicitors when preparing their Form E. In those instances, the member should be advised that a formal CETV is required and asked to obtain one from Veterans UK, ideally a more comprehensive paid-for CETV, to ensure that the correct information is provided to the court and the benefits statement not used.

When instructing a PODE in relation to an armed forces scheme it is necessary to include the member's anticipated retirement date so that the PODE is able to properly calculate the anticipated income in retirement, otherwise incorrect assumptions could be made which would impact the report's figures. For example, if a member is due to retire prior to their normal retirement and EDP will be payable but excluded from the income figures, this should be noted in the LOI.

In the event that a pension sharing order is ordered/agreed, it is necessary to prepare a pension sharing annex for each pension scheme that is being shared. Each pension scheme (1975, 2005, 2015) is treated individually by Veterans UK when sharing a pension, which means that each pension being shared also attracts a fee. This is often the case with public sector pensions and the same applies to the NHS who also require one annex per scheme. The current fee schedule for AFPS pensions is available on the gov.uk website. An AFPS pension sharing credit cannot be transferred out of the AFPS pension scheme, the pension credit is transferred into a pension pot in the non-member spouse's name, independently of the member spouse. It is not necessary to tick the relevant box on the pension sharing annex to implement this, which in any event should be avoided at all costs as per *T v T*.

AFPS pension schemes, along with all other public sector pension scheme, do not allow external transfers to schemes that provide "flexible benefits", which is the ability to take the money from a pension as cash (pension freedoms). This is set out in the Pensions Schemes Act 2015 s.68, which amended s.95 of the Pension Schemes Act 1993. s.95(2A) of the Pension Schemes Act 1993 and confirms that you cannot transfer benefits from an unfunded public sector scheme, which the AFPS pension schemes are, into a scheme that allows flexible benefits. A member could transfer it into another defined benefit scheme, such as the NHS for example, but not into a defined contribution scheme that allows a member to take the cash out.

Because of the different rules surrounding each scheme, they also each have different rules on when a pension credit member is able to receive their benefits, and what those benefits are. The pension credit member will receive their pension benefits when they reach the scheme's deferred pension age, which is state retirement age for the 2015 scheme, 65 for the 2005 scheme and 60/65 for the 1975 scheme. If the 1975 or 2005 pensions are shared, then a lump sum will also be payable when the pension comes into payment, but only if the pension-member has not already had the lump sum. If a member of the armed forces has retired and received their tax-free lump sum prior to the implementation of the pension sharing order, the non-member spouse will not then receive a lump sum when the pension comes into payment. The serving spouse should be advised that their lump sum is not treated separately from their pension income prior to it being paid out, and if they will receive a lower pension income as a result of a pension sharing order, then their lump sum will also be reduced. This should be set out in the PODE report with an illustration of their anticipated income.

The pension is not paid automatically to the pension credit member; it must be applied for. A pension credit member is able to receive their pension early though, as early as age 55 on all schemes. However, the Veterans UK Pension Benefits on Divorce and Dissolution of Civil Partnerships guidance confirms that in those cases, the amount of income paid will be reduced as the pension is being paid out for longer. In those cases where it is intended that the pension will be taken early, the PODE should be made aware of this, and the calculation date should be that earlier date. Do not assume that just because a pension member is in receipt of their pension that the pension credit member will also receive their pension income immediately if they are younger than the scheme's deferred pension age as they will not.

As with any pension sharing order, the value of the pension credit is calculated on the day that the pension provider implements the pension sharing order. With armed forces pensions this could be a significant difference if the serving member is promoted during the divorce proceedings or passes their immediate pension point as this could significantly change the value of their pension and the benefits that will be paid. In those instances, and if practitioners or a party are aware of a potential change, then an updated CETV and PODE calculations may be required otherwise it could result in an incorrect amount of pension being shared. It would be wise to check the serving members dates of service and the scheme rules to see if the immediate pension point is passed.

This is a broad overview of a very complex pension scheme and has only addressed pensions applicable to regular serving members.

There are separate schemes for reservists and different rules applicable to those in receipt of an ill-health pension or those were medically discharged. There is a wide range of information available on the gov.uk website which explains the pension types and each of the schemes' respective rules, features and benefits and specialist financial advice would be a sensible step to ensure that the client is properly advised. Practitioners who encounter AFPS pensions should ensure that these guides are reviewed to familiarise themselves with each scheme, though be mindful that financial advice should not be given to clients on how to deal with their pensions. PODE input is almost always necessary for these types of schemes given their unique features.

Whilst this information has related to armed forces pensions, the basic principles are very similar across most public sector pensions. Each scheme has its own rules and publishes its own online guidance, and this should be checked when these pensions arise.

CHAPTER SEVEN

MCCLOUD

The McCloud case has become almost infamous for anyone who has or is involved with, public sector pensions. The case came about as a result of the reforms to public sector pensions implemented in 2015. The government had sought to change the way that public sector pensions were funded, and Lord Hutton was commission to prepare a report on the matter, which was published in 2011. The outcome of his report was a recommendation to close the existing final salary schemes (known as legacy schemes) and instead move public sector workers onto a new pension scheme. The result of this report was the Public Service Pensions Act 2013 which changes the pensions for the following class of public sector workers, as per s.1(2) of the Act:

- civil servants;
- The judiciary;
- Local government workers for England, Wales and Scotland;
- Teachers for England, Wales and Scotland;
- Health service workers for England, Wales and Scotland;
- Fire and rescue workers for England, Wales and Scotland;
- Members of police forces for England, Wales and Scotland;

- The armed forces.

The Act stipulated that there were to be no new members enrolled in the previous schemes or contributions paid into them for service after 31 March 2014 for local government schemes, or 31 March 2015 for all other schemes such as Firefighters, NHS and the armed forces (s.18(4)) and from that date all members would either be enrolled, or their continued service would result in accrual under the new schemes. The act enabled scheme regulators to exclude certain members from this legislation by virtue of subsection 5 if they were members of the earlier scheme before 1 April 2012 and specifically used the example in subsection 6 of a member attaining their normal retirement age by a certain date. This legislation enabled scheme administrators to permit some members to stay in the legacy schemes until they retired, and this was based on their age. If a member was within 10 years of their normal retirement age, then they did not have to enrol in the 2015 schemes. Some pension schemes, including the NHS and Firefighters also introduced "tapered protection" for their members, again based on age.

As a result of this piece of legislation, Judges and Firefighters brought proceedings in, initially, the Employment Tribunal against the government and pension scheme administrators on the grounds that they were directly discriminated against based on their age, and indirectly discriminated against based on race and sex. The Judge's case was McCloud and the Firefighters case was known as Sargeant. The case was appealed from the Employment Tribunal to the Court of Appeal, who gave their judgement in November 2018. The Court of Appeal ([2018] EWCA Civ 2844) adopted the same view that the transitional protections were discriminatory. Permission to appeal to the Supreme Court was refused in June 2019, with the government releasing a statement in July 2019 confirming that the "government will be engaging with employer and member representatives", with the matter being sent back to the Employment Tribunal to determine a remedy.

Eventually, in February 2021, the government announced how the discrimination would be remedied. In the government's response to the consultation, "Public service pension schemes: changes to the transitional arrangements to the 2015 schemes" Steve Barclay MP, Chief Secretary to the Treasury, confirmed that "*the government intends to proceed with the deferred choice underpin. This means that members will make their decision between scheme benefits shortly before benefits are paid from the scheme. In the meantime, members will be deemed to have accrued benefits in their legacy schemes, rather than reformed schemes, for the remedy period, until they make that choice*". A member will then be able to choose which scheme is most favourable to them when they retire, rather than trying to second guess now what will be the most financially favourable outcome to them when they retire in the future. Pension members will be able to weigh up their options, consider both retaining their pension benefits under the legacy schemes or transferring them to the 2015 scheme and take whichever one is best for them financially.

The legacy schemes closed to all members from 31 March 2022 and from that point on all members have accrued rights in the 2015 scheme regardless of their age or length of service. The date that the discrimination occurred is 1 April 2015 to 31 March 2022, and members who had earlier pension schemes prior to the 2015 revisions may benefit from the deferred choice underpin when they come to take their benefits. It is important not to assume that a member will be better off taking their benefits under the earlier scheme than the 2015 scheme as it varies for each individual based on their pension scheme and the schemes rules and practitioners cannot advise their client of this as it could constitute financial advice.

The government consultation considered the effect that this would also have on divorced pension members who had a pension credit. They themselves were not discriminated against as they were not the pension member, with the government confirming that they will not have the opportunity to elect which pension scheme their benefits are attributed to. Instead, the government have confirmed that *"the pension credit member will be awarded the percentage (as specified by the courts) of the higher cash equivalent transfer value (CETV) due under remedy; this will not be changed to reflect any choice the scheme member [here the pension debit member] makes, which would result in a lower pension amount."* This confirms that a pension debit member cannot cause their former spouse to receive a lesser pension income by the choice that they make when they receive their pension benefits and make their election under the deferred choice underpin. What may be more financially viable for the pension debit member may not also be beneficial for the pension credit member who receives the pension sharing order, and they will be kept entirely independent of one another.

However, this inevitably does have an impact on an affected member who is divorcing. First, consider whether the party is a member of one of the affected schemes. Those impacted must have been members of the scheme on or before 31 March 2012 and continued beyond 1 April 2015, when the revised pension scheme came in and be a member of the 2015 pension scheme. This will require clarification of the pension members dates of service/employment when looking at their relevant pension through checking employment dates on their CETV, or their Form E. Once it has been established that a member is one of those who has the benefit of the McCloud judgement it would be prudent to bring this to the PODE's attention when preparing the letter of instruction in the event that it impacts on their calculations.

The government has now started corresponding with members who are impacted by McCould. For members of the armed forces, those who are currently serving were automatically returned to the "legacy Scheme" for the relevant period. They will receive an "information only" Remedial Service Statement (RSS) which sets out their current pensions benefits with a comparison of their benefits were they to elect to have their pensions for the remedy period reverted to the "legacy benefits" on retirement. Those members do not need to take any action, but the RSS should be provided with the letter of instruction to the PODE so that appropriate consideration can be given when preparing the report.

Those who are in receipt of their pensions will receive an RSS that requires them to make an election of whether to remain on the 2015 benefits for the remedy period, or whether to revert to the earlier scheme. It is not a given that the legacy benefits were better, and it comes down to each individual based on their careers. If a pension member has made an election under McCloud, this should also be conveyed to the PODE. For those who have received their RSS but not yet made the election, this information should again be provided to the PODE with the LOI. guidance issued by the government in February 2015 states that *"Due to technical challenges we are not able to guarantee all members will receive their RSS by 01 April 2025 as originally planned. We now plan for all members to have received their RSS by 30 September 2025."* There are clearly ongoing delays, and this is a continuously evolving situation. Practitioners should find out from pension members what the position is with their RSS, whether they have received one and whether they have made an election.

This situation is constantly evolving and practitioners who are involved in cases with affected public services pensions should continue to research the respective schemes responses to McCloud for further updates and ensure that necessary questions are asked of PODEs when expert reports are prepared. Pension scheme administrators are generally sending out guidance notes with CETVs and these should be read carefully for up-to-date information.

CHAPTER EIGHT

CONCLUSION

Pensions on divorce is a wide ranging and multi-faceted area of law. It is also an evolving area of law, with pension sharing orders only coming into law in the early 2000s, comparatively recently in comparison to the majority of divorce and financial remedy black letter law from the 1970s. It has progressed from pensions being treated simply as any other capital asset and being offset accordingly, to cases where a PODE report has become the norm in the majority of cases.

Practitioners should be alert to the issue of pensions from the earliest stage in a matter, not only to ensure that the correct advice is given but also to ensure that the timetable for a matter and of course the expectations of our clients, is managed appropriately. Adding pensions into a divorce as an issue to be determined almost invariable leads to a matter taking longer than it would without them. A party who wants a "quick" divorce is not going to be find that an outcome where information from pension providers/employers is required, or a PODE report is necessary. That is in no way a reflection on the PODEs, but simply a reflection of the complex calculations they are asked to provide and the time that it takes for the information to be obtained.

Financial disclosure is a key aspect. The better the disclosure at the outset the more likely a case is to progress smoothly, and time invested in the beginning to obtain the relevant information will pay dividends later in the process. Ensure that the CETV is obtained for each and every pension, ask the client to think back over their employment history and make enquiries as to whether they may have had a pension. That brief spell with a large national bank in the 1980s may have left them with a defined benefit pension, as was common at the time, that they didn't know they had. Whether it is to be included in any pension sharing order or calculation on divorce is a different matter, but to comply with a party's duty of ongoing financial disclosure the information must be provided.

Upon receipt of disclosure a thorough analysis of the Form E and the CETV should be caried out. Check that the Form E has been properly completed and that the information on the CETV matches, as well as properly checking the type of pension. Defined benefit or defined contribution could have a material impact on the course of a matter and whether further expert input is necessary, or whether it is a matter where there could be an offsetting calculation done instead.

It is now commonplace to instruct a PODE to properly report on a pension. In those instances where PODE input is required, the letter of instruction should be drafted thoroughly and with appropriate thought given to the dates being used for calculations. If in court proceedings, finalise the letter of instruction as much as possible prior to and at the FDA. The more "to be agreed..." aspects of the letter of instruction there are the greater the scope for disagreement after the FDA, leading to increased costs and delay. It may be prudent to ask the FDA judge to order the inclusion of additional calculation dates to cater for extra-marital pension contributions as it may not be a matter that will be willingly agreed by the party looking to obtain a pension sharing order. It may be considered appropriate to have that information before the court so that the court can give an indication at the FDR and any suggestion at that early stage that pre-marital pensions are to be included could be said to be pre-determining the outcome. By way of compromise, it may be necessary that a party who wishes to have those additional calculations prepared has to bear the costs of them in the first instance.

For those resolving a dispute using NCDR, if possible try to work with your mediator to agree the scope of the instructions to go in the LOI, with the parties then seeking their own independent legal advice. Hybrid-mediation, with solicitors present, may help facilitate quicker discussions about the scope of the report and avoid undue delays or wrangling over the terms.

With the letter of instruction finalised, the dates for equalisation etc agreed, consider the deadline for the report. Ensure that the PODE can report in time for the FDR, and do not make assumptions that they will report to a court deadline as that may simply not be possible. If a report cannot be prepared in time, then it makes an FDR ineffective, leading to potential costs consequences if there is blame to be attributable to a party. Time to gather the relevant date should also be factored into the timetable as that is easy to overlook and invariably results in the PODE being pushed to report by a certain deadline or not in time at all.

Practitioners who find themselves dealing with public sector pensions in light of McCloud should continue to be alert to the remedy provided by the government and whether the member has received their RSS or, if they have retired, made an election for their McCloud remedy. Whilst they may have confirmed that deferred choice underpin is the way to remedy the discrimination, how this plays out in practice and what impact it actually has on a pension remains to be seen for many cases, or until a member reaches their retirement age and is given the choice.

Once the report is received, consider it carefully. Review it in line with the recent case law and the client's stated aims and objectives, focussing of course on whether the proposed outcome from the PODE ensures that needs are met. Consider the age of the parties and their other assets, how does the value of their pensions fit into the context of the asset base? If it is small in comparison then it may not be considered, in the context of the parties' needs, as significant as it would in a small low to medium value case where there are no alternative sources of income in retirement. Is one party retaining a portfolio of buy to let properties to generate an income or that could be sold to release capital in retirement but still insisting on a pension sharing order to equalise retirement income? Is that fair in the circumstances? These are all factors to be considered when reviewing the report, often the last piece of information received before pre-FDR offers are made and should be considered as part of the s.25 MCA criteria.

When it comes to proposals and submissions at a final hearing, look to the case law and consider your arguments carefully. Offsetting is not the favoured approach in pension, and neither is ring fencing pensions. If you act for a party with significant pre-marital pension contributions, then submissions should be made akin to those made when trying to ring-fence other non-matrimonial property and try and persuade the court that the other party's needs will be met without requiring recourse to non-matrimonial pension assets. Whilst it may be a difficult task now, it is still a point that can be advanced if the facts of the case lend themselves to it, younger parties without children who are divorcing after a short marriage by way of example. As with any financial remedy case, the individual facts of the case are determinative of how it will be treated, and as is often the case in an area of law that is so heavily based on judicial discretion, what one judge considers a fair outcome may not be the same as the way another judge would decide it.

The latest approach to the treatment of pensions on divorce has been to treat them as a separate asset from other capital. That has been covered numerous times in case law and academic discussions, and it appears that there is now a way forward on that point. As before, it does very much depend on the circumstances of a case, but certainly cases involving large public sector pensions or other defined benefit schemes should approach a pension as an entirely separate asset from other capital and not be tempted to simply offset it with other capital assets, the result could be detrimental to a client and potentially negligent on the practitioner's part.

As with any element of financial remedy cases, if there is ever doubt or uncertainty on the practitioner's part, defer to the appropriate expert. A financial advisor can give advice on the most appropriate means of investing a pension credit, or the means by which to release cash from a pension under the pension freedom rules in such a way as to avoid a large tax liability. A PODE will ensure that proper calculations are completed to enable a pension to be split to achieve equal income in retirement or give a figure for offsetting that can be used for proceedings. Where there are concerns about the CETV and whether it accurately represents the value of a pension member's benefits under a scheme, a PODE will be able to provide a fair actuarial value/market consistent valuation of the pension.

MORE BOOKS BY LAW BRIEF PUBLISHING

A selection of our other titles available now:-

'The Electronic Communications Code: A Practical Guide – Second Edition' by Kerry Bretherton KC, James Castle, Mark Loveday
'A Practical Guide to the Independent School Standards – September 2023 Edition' by Sarah McKimm
'A Practical Guide to Estate Administration and Crypto Assets' by Richard Marshall
'A Practical Guide to Parental Alienation in Private and Public Law Children Cases' by Sam King QC & Frankie Shama
'Contested Heritage – Removing Art from Land and Historic Buildings' by Richard Harwood QC, Catherine Dobson, David Sawtell
'The Limits of Separate Legal Personality: When Those Running a Company Can Be Held Personally Liable for Losses Caused to Third Parties Outside of the Company' by Dr Mike Wilkinson
'A Practical Guide to Transgender Law' by Robin Moira White & Nicola Newbegin
'A Practical Guide to 'Stranded Spouses' in Family Law' by Mani Singh Basi
'A Practical Guide to Residential Freehold Conveyancing' by Lorraine Richardson
'A Practical Guide to Pensions on Divorce for Lawyers' by Bryan Scant
'A Practical Guide to Challenging Sham Marriage Allegations in Immigration Law' by Priya Solanki
'A Practical Guide to Digital Communications Evidence in Criminal Law' by Sam Willis
'A Practical Guide to Legal Rights in Scotland' by Sarah-Jane Macdonald
'A Practical Guide to New Build Conveyancing' by Paul Sams & Rebecca East
'A Practical Guide to Inherited Wealth on Divorce' by Hayley Trim
'A Practical Guide to Practice Direction 12J and Domestic Abuse in Private Law Children Proceedings' by Rebecca Cross & Malvika Jaganmohan
'A Practical Guide to Confiscation and Restraint' by Narita Bahra QC, John Carl Townsend, David Winch
'A Practical Guide to the Law of Forests in Scotland' by Philip Buchan
'A Practical Guide to Health and Medical Cases in Immigration Law' by Rebecca Chapman & Miranda Butler
'A Practical Guide to Bad Character Evidence for Criminal Practitioners by Aparna Rao
'A Practical Guide to Extradition Law post-Brexit' by Myles Grandison et al
'A Practical Guide to Hoarding and Mental Health for Housing Lawyers' by Rachel Coyle

'Stephens on Contractual Indemnities' by Richard Stephens
'A Practical Guide to the EU Succession Regulation' by Richard Frimston
'A Practical Guide to Solicitor and Client Costs – Second Edition' by Robin Dunne
'Constructive Dismissal – Practice Pointers and Principles' by Benjimin Burgher
'A Practical Guide to Religion and Belief Discrimination Claims in the Workplace' by Kashif Ali
'A Practical Guide to the Law of Medical Treatment Decisions' by Ben Troke
'Fundamental Dishonesty and QOCS in Personal Injury Proceedings: Law and Practice' by Jake Rowley
'A Practical Guide to the Law in Relation to School Exclusions' by Charlotte Hadfield & Alice de Coverley
'A Practical Guide to Divorce for the Silver Separators' by Karin Walker
'The Right to be Forgotten – The Law and Practical Issues' by Melissa Stock
'A Practical Guide to Planning Law and Rights of Way in National Parks, the Broads and AONBs' by James Maurici QC, James Neill et al
'A Practical Guide to Election Law' by Tom Tabori
'A Practical Guide to the Law in Relation to Surrogacy' by Andrew Powell
'A Practical Guide to Claims Arising from Fatal Accidents – Second Edition' by James Patience
'A Practical Guide to Asbestos Claims' by Jonathan Owen & Gareth McAloon
'A Practical Guide to Stamp Duty Land Tax in England and Northern Ireland' by Suzanne O'Hara
'A Practical Guide to the Law of Farming Partnerships' by Philip Whitcomb
'A Practical Guide to the Law of Unlawful Eviction and Harassment – Second Edition' by Stephanie Lovegrove
'A Practical Guide to Costs in Personal Injury Claims – Second Edition' by Matthew Hoe
'A Practical Guide to the General Data Protection Regulation (GDPR) – Second Edition' by Keith Markham
'A Practical Guide to Working with Litigants in Person and McKenzie Friends in Family Cases' by Stuart Barlow
'Protecting Unregistered Brands: A Practical Guide to the Law of Passing Off' by Lorna Brazell
'A Practical Guide to Secondary Liability and Joint Enterprise Post-Jogee' by Joanne Cecil & James Mehigan

'A Practical Guide to the Pre-Action RTA Claims Protocol for Personal Injury Lawyers' by Antonia Ford

'A Practical Guide to Neighbour Disputes and the Law' by Alexander Walsh

'A Practical Guide to Coercive Control for Legal Practitioners and Victims' by Rachel Horman

'A Practical Guide to the Law of Driverless Cars – Second Edition'

by Alex Glassbrook, Emma Northey & Scarlett Milligan

'A Practical Guide to TOLATA Claims' by Greg Williams

'A Practical Guide to Elderly Law – Second Edition' by Justin Patten

'A Practical Guide to Responding to Housing Disrepair and Unfitness Claims' by Iain Wightwick

'A Practical Guide to the Law of Bullying and Harassment in the Workplace' by Philip Hyland

'How to Be a Freelance Solicitor: A Practical Guide to the SRA-Regulated Freelance Solicitor Model' by Paul Bennett

'A Practical Guide to Prison Injury Claims' by Malcolm Johnson

'A Practical Guide to Advising Clients at the Police Station' by Colin Stephen McKeown-Beaumont

'A Practical Guide to Antisocial Behaviour Injunctions – Second Edition' by Iain Wightwick

'Practical Mediation: A Guide for Mediators, Advocates, Advisers, Lawyers, and Students in Civil, Commercial, Business, Property, Workplace, and Employment Cases' by Jonathan Dingle with John Sephton

'The Mini-Pupillage Workbook' by David Boyle

'A Practical Guide to Crofting Law' by Brian Inkster

'A Practical Guide to the Law of Domain Names and Cybersquatting' by Andrew Clemson

'A Practical Guide to the Law of Gender Pay Gap Reporting' by Harini Iyengar

'NHS Whistleblowing and the Law' by Joseph England

'Employment Law and the Gig Economy' by Nigel Mackay & Annie Powell

'A Practical Guide to Noise Induced Hearing Loss (NIHL) Claims' by Andrew Mckie, Ian Skeate, Gareth McAloon

'An Introduction to Beauty Negligence Claims – A Practical Guide for the Personal Injury Practitioner' by Greg Almond

'Intercompany Agreements for Transfer Pricing Compliance' by Paul Sutton

'Zen and the Art of Mediation' by Martin Plowman

'A Practical Guide to Adoption for Family Lawyers' by Graham Pegg

'A Practical Guide to Industrial Disease Claims' by Andrew Mckie & Ian Skeate
'A Practical Guide to Conducting a Sheriff Court Proof' by Andrew Stevenson
'A Practical Guide to Vicarious Liability' by Mariel Irvine
'A Practical Guide to Applications for Landlord's Consent and Variation of Leases' by Mark Shelton
'A Practical Guide to Relief from Sanctions Post-Mitchell and Denton' by Peter Causton
'A Practical Guide to Equity Release for Advisors' by Paul Sams
'A Practical Guide to Financial Services Claims' by Chris Hegarty
'A Practical Guide to Financial Ombudsman Service Claims' by Adam Temple & Robert Scrivenor
'A Practical Guide to Running Housing Disrepair and Cavity Wall Claims – Second Edition' by Andrew Mckie & Ian Skeate
'A Practical Guide to Holiday Sickness Claims – Second Edition' by Andrew Mckie & Ian Skeate
'Arguments and Tactics for Personal Injury and Clinical Negligence Claims' by Dorian Williams
'A Practical Guide to Drone Law' by Rufus Ballaster, Andrew Firman, Eleanor Clot
'On Experts: CPR35 for Lawyers and Experts' by David Boyle
'An Introduction to Personal Injury Law' by David Boyle

www.ingramcontent.com/pod-product-compliance
Lightning Source LLC
LaVergne TN
LVHW022306200926
848481LV00004B/1234
* 9 7 8 1 9 1 8 2 4 1 0 9 9 *